The Jesus Story

Musings For Meditation And Application

John Sawyer

Parson's Porch Books
www.parsonsporchbooks.com

The Jesus Story: Musings For Meditation And Application
ISBN: Softcover 978-1-949888-43-0
Copyright © 2018 by John Sawyer

All rights reserved. No part of this book may be reproduced or transmitted in any form or by any means, electronic or mechanical, including photocopying, recording, or by any information storage and retrieval system, without permission in writing from the publisher.

Cover Credit - *Christus Pantocrator* - Artistic representation of Jesus Christ God, the second divine Person of the Most Holy Trinity (Cathedral of Cefalù, c. 1130.)

The Jesus Story

Contents

Foreword 13

Introduction 15

The Angel's Visit to Zechariah 21
    Luke 1:5-25; 57-80

The Angel's Visit to Mary 24
    Luke 1:26-56

The Birth of Jesus 27
    Luke 2:1-38; Matthew 1:18-25

The Visit of the Wise Men 30
    Matthew 2:1-12

The Childhood of Jesus 33
    Matthew 2:13-23; Luke 2:39-52

The Baptism and Temptations of Jesus 39
    Matthew 3:1-17; 4:1-11; Mark 1:1-13;
    Luke 3:1-38; 4:1-13; John 1:19-34

Jesus Called His First Disciples 42
    John 1:35-51

Jesus Performed His First Miracle 45
    John 2:1-12

Jesus Cleansed the Temple 48
    John 2:13-22

Jesus Met with Nicodemus 51
    John 2:23-25; 3:1-21

Jesus Met the Samaritan Woman 54
    John 3:22-36; 4:1-42

Jesus Healed the Nobleman's Son 58
    Matthew 4:17; Mark 1:14-15
    Luke 4:14-15; John 4:46-54

Jesus Rejected at Nazareth 62
    Matthew 4:13-16; Luke 4:16-31

Jesus Called Four Disciples 64
    Matthew 4:18-22; Mark 1:16-20; Luke 5:1-11

Jesus Healed a Demoniac in the Synagogue 67
    Mark 1:21-28; Luke 4:31-37

Jesus Healed Simon Peter's Mother-in-Law: 70
    Matthew 8:14-17; Mark 1:29-39; Luke 4:38-44

Jesus Healed a Leper 73
    Matthew 8:1-4; Mark 1:40-45; Luke 5:12-16
    Matthew 9:1-8; Mark 2:1-12; Luke 5:17-26

Jesus Healed a Paralytic 76
    Matthew 9:1-8; Mark 2:1-12; Luke 5:17-26

Jesus Called Levi 78
    Matthew 9:9-17; Mark 2:13-22; Luke 5:27-39

Jesus Healed a Lame Man 81
    John 5:1-47

Jesus Healed a Man with a Shriveled Hand 83
    Matthew 12:15-21; Mark 3:1-6; Luke 6:6-11

Jesus Selected 12 Apostles 85
    Matthew 10:1-4; Mark 3:7-19; Luke 6:12-16

Jesus Gave the Sermon on the Mount 88
    Matthew 5:1-48; 6:1-34; 7:1-29; Luke 6:17-49

Jesus Healed a Centurion's Servant 91
    Matthew 8:5-13; Luke 7:1-10
Jesus Raised a Widow's Son from the Dead 94
    Luke 7:11-17
Jesus Was Anointed by a Sinful Woman 96
    Luke 7:36-50
Jesus Healed a Blind and Mute Man 99
    Matthew 12:22-43; Mark 3:19-30
Jesus' Mother and Brothers Tried to Take Jesus Home 101
    Matthew 12:46-50; Mark 3:31-35; Luke 8:19-21
Jesus Taught by Parables 103
    Matthew 13:1-58; Mark 4:1-34; Luke 8:1-18
Jesus Stilled the Storm at Sea 105
    Matthew 8:18-27; Mark 4:35-41; Luke 8:22-25
Jesus Healed the Gerasene Demoniacs 107
    Matthew 8:28-34; Mark 5:1-20; Luke 8:26-39
Jesus Healed the Woman with an Issue of Blood 110
    Matthew 9:20-22; Mark 5:21-34; Luke 8:43-48
Jesus Raised Jairus' Daughter from the Dead 113
    Matthew 9:18-26; Mark 5:21-43; Luke 8:40-56
Jesus Healed Two Blind Men and A Man Who Was Mute 116
    Matthew 9:27-34; 13:54-58; Mark 6:1-6
Jesus Sent Out 70 Disciples 119
    Matthew 9:35-38; 10:1-42; 11:1
    Mark 6:6-13; Luke 9:1-6

Jesus Fed More Than 5,000 People 122
    Matthew 14:13-21; Mark 6:30-44
    Luke 9:10-17; John 6:1-13
Jesus Walked on the Water 125
    Matthew 14:22-36; Mark 6:45-56
    John 6:14-21
Jesus Did Not Conform to People's Expectations 127
    Matthew 15:1-20; Mark 7:1-23
    John 6:22-71; 7:1
Jesus Healed The Daughter Of A Syrian-Phonenic Woman 130
    Matthew 15:21-28; Mark 7:24-30
Jesus Healed a Deaf Man and Fed More than 4,000 People 133
    Matthew 15:29-38; Mark 7:31-37; 8:1-9
Jesus Healed a Blind Man in Bethsaida 136
    Matthew 15:39; 16:1-12; Mark 8:10-26
Jesus Taught His Disciples at Caesarea Philippi 139
    Matthew 16:13-28; Mark 8:27-38; Luke 9:18-27
Jesus Was Transfigured 142
    Matthew 17:1-113; Mark 9:1-13; Luke 9:28-36
Jesus Healed a Demoniac Boy 145
    Matthew 17:14-20; Mark 9:14-29; Luke 9: 37-43
Jesus Taught at the Feast of Tabernacles 148
    John 7:11-52
Jesus Forgave the Woman Caught in Adultery 150
    John 7:53; 8:1-59
Jesus Healed a Blind Man 153
    John 9:1-41;

Jesus Sent Out 70 Disciples 155
    Luke 10:1-24
Jesus Told About the Good Samaritan 158
    Luke 10:25-37
Jesus Healed a Mute Man 161
    Luke 11:1-36
Jesus Told About a Rich Fool 164
    Luke 12:1-59
Jesus Healed a Woman Who Was Bent Over 167
    Luke 13:1-21
Jesus Dined with A Pharisee and Healed A Man 173
    Luke 14:1-25; Luke 15:1-32
Jesus Told About the Prodigal Son 175
    Luke 15:1-32
Jesus Told About the Rich Man and Lazarus 177
    Luke 16:1-31
Jesus Raised Lazarus from the Dead 179
    John 11:1-57
Jesus Healed 10 Lepers 182
    Luke 17:11-37
Met with the Rich Young Ruler 184
    Matthew 19:16-30; Mark 10:17-31; Luke 18:18-30
Jesus Healed Bartimaeus and His Companion 187
    Matthew 20:17-34; Mark 10:32-52; Luke 18:31-43
Jesus Goes Home with Zacchaeus 190
    Luke 19:1-28

Jesus' Triumphal Entry into Jerusalem 194
    Matthew 21:1-17; Mark 11:1-11
    Luke 19:29-44; John 11:55-57; 12:1-19

Jesus Cleansed the Temple a Second Time 198
    Matthew 21:12-13; Mark 11:12-18; Luke 19:45-48

Some Greeks Want to See Jesus 201
    John 12:20-50

The Rulers Tried to Trap Jesus 204
    Matthew 21:23-46; 22:1-46
    Mark 11:27-33; 12:1-10; Luke 20:1-47

Jesus Taught His Disciples on the Mount of Olives 207
    Matthew24:1-51; 25:1-46; Mark 13:1-37
    Luke 21:1-38

Jerusalem Jesus Ate with Simon the Leper 210
    Matthew 26:6-13; Mark 14:3-9; John 12:2-8

Jesus' Last Meal with His Disciples 213
    Matthew 26:17-30; Mark 14:12-26
    Luke 22:7-38; John 13:1-38; 14:1-31

Jesus in the Garden of Gethsemane 219
    Matthew26:30-46; Mark 14:26-42
    Luke 22:39-46 John 18:1

Jesus Was Betrayed and Arrested 221
    Matthew 26:47-56; Mark 14:43-52
    Luke 22:47-53; John 18:2-12

Jesus Before Annas and the Sanhedrin 224
    Matthew 26:57-75; Mark 14:53-75
    Luke 22:54-71; John 18:12-27

Jesus Before Governor Pilate 227
    Matthew 27:1-26; Mark 15:1-15
    Luke 23:1-25; John 18:28-40; 19:1-16

Jesus Was Led to Golgotha 230
    Matthew 27:27-34; Mark 15:16-23
    Luke 23:26-32; John 19:17

Jesus on the Cross 232
    Matthew 27:35-56; Mark 15: 24-41
    Luke 23:33-49; John 19:31-42

Jesus Was Buried 235
    Matthew 27:57-66; Mark 15:42-47
    Luke 23:50-56; John 19:31-42

Women Came to Jesus' Tomb 237
    Matthew 28:1-15; Mark 16:1-11
    Luke 24:1-12; John 20:1-18

Jesus Appeared to Two Disciples on the Road to Emmaus 241
    Mark 16:12-13; Luke 24:13-35

Jesus Appeared to the Disciples 245
    Mark 16:14; Luke 24:36-40; John 20:19-31

Jesus Met with Seven Disciples at the Sea of Galilee 247
    John 21:1-26

Jesus Met with Over 500 Believers in Galilee 249
    Matthew 28:16-20; Mark 16:15-18;
    I Corinthians 15:6

Jesus Ascended to Heaven 252
    Mark 16:19-20; Luke 24:50-53; Acts 1:9-12

Foreword

Three years ago, a longtime friend of mine, Dr. Arthur Crisco, asked me to do some volunteer writing for a Christian mission organization, for which he is the volunteer editor. Art requested me to write eighty short pieces on what he called *The Jesus Story*. The outline came from Dr. A.T. Robertson's *Harmony of the Gospels*. The eighty writings were going to be put into leaflet form. They were to be simple, for persons who may have never heard of Jesus or possess a Bible. When I completed the assignment, Art suggested that I put them in book form for use as a personal devotional or study guide for groups. The following pages are the result..

By the way, this is not required reading and you certainly do not have to agree with me.

Dr. Crisco requested that all the Scripture quoted be from the New International Version. I think I did that, though some may be my preference, New Revised Standard Version.

The Bible is a very special book, but a very dangerous book. It has been used to support, slavery, racism, sexism, commercialism, capitalism, and all manner of isms and corruption. Individuals, churches and governments have been guilty, not to mention a host of preachers. But the Bible has also helped to change millions of lives for the better.

In my opinion, the entire Bible should be interpreted in the light of what we know and understand about the life and teachings of Jesus. With that in mind, it is my prayer that you will enjoy and be blessed as you work your way through the Jesus Story as told by the four Gospel writers. Please take time to read the scripture passages before reading my notes and application suggestions. Try to read the scripture as though it was your first time. Do not hurry. Take time to think. The material was written for individual or group study, meditation and application. It was written with hope that you will think for yourself. Draw your own conclusions. And work toward becoming a mature person.

John Sawyer

October 15, 2018

Introduction
John 1:1-18

As an introduction to the story of Jesus as told in all four of the Gospels, we are using a study of John 1:1-18. The Gospels are the first four books in The New Testament of the Christian Bible. They are Matthew, Mark, Luke and John.

This study follows the outline of A.T. Robertson's book, *A Harmony of the Gospels*. It was his attempt to put the events and teachings of Jesus life in chronological order. It should be noted that there are differences of opinion about chronology even by the gospel writers themselves. For example; Matthew puts the Sermon on the Mount (a well-known passage) near the beginning of Jesus ministry. Luke puts his version much later. Jesus message at his home synagogue (place of Jewish study and worship) is near the beginning of Luke, but later in Matthew.

The purpose of the writers was not to write biography with exact time and place but to tell the story of Jesus in a convincing and truthful way to the people and churches. Keep in mind that most of the people probably could not read. They would hear the stories read inhouse churches or maybe in homes of those who could afford a copy and could read.

Mark is believed to be the first written, perhaps between 60 and 70 A.D., or about thirty to forty years after what is written about occurred. Matthew and Luke seem to follow Mark and contain nearly everything that Mark wrote. They can be dated from about 70-90 A.D. Because so much of their material is the same, these three are called the synoptic gospels. Synoptic means to see with or see together. John, as you will see, is very different and probably written between 90 and 100 A.D. Two of the writers were among the "twelve disciples" of Jesus. They were Matthew and John. Luke may have not been a Jew. Mark was the son of Mary, a follower of Jesus from Jerusalem. He is also called John Mark.

Jesus is the central figure in history. The gospels are our main source of written information about Jesus. So, in the study of the Bible as a whole, the life and teaching of Jesus is the standard by which all other scripture is tested. That is, do the words or events carry the spirit of love and compassion of Jesus. Example. Slavery and war are often justified because the people of the Bible had slaves and fought a whole lot. Neither can stand before the life and teachings of Jesus.

Volumes have been written on the passage for this lesson (John 1:1-18). It is called "The Prologue" to John's gospel. And we are using it to introduce the study of all four gospels. It is so different from the beginning of the others. You may take time to read and study each verse. Space prohibits such a study in this lesson.

"In the beginning was the Word, and the Word was with God, and the Word was God." Many believe John is using the word 'logos' translated Word to speak to both Jews and Greeks. In verse 9 he changes metaphor from Word to light. "The true light that gives light to everyone was coming into the world."

Who is this Word, this light? Look at verse 14. "The Word became flesh and made his dwelling among us." The Creator, verse 3, became a part of the creation. The divine became human. But why? The book of Hebrews 4:14 -15 (in The New Testament) says: "Therefore, since we have a great high priest who has ascended into heaven, Jesus the Son of God, let us hold firmly to the faith we profess. For we do not have a high priest who is unable to empathize with our weaknesses, but we have one who has been tempted in every way, just as we are—yet he did not sin." God took on flesh to show what life means.

John's gospel in verse 9 of chapter 14 Jesus said: "Anyone who has seen me has seen the Father (God)."

Jesus came to show us what God is like. So, we have the story of Jesus who is human but divine. He shows us, even unto death by execution by the earthly powers that be, that God loves and forgives us. And he shows and teaches us how to live as those who love God. "No one has ever seen God, but the one and only Son, who is himself God and in the closest relationship with the Father, has made him known." John 1:18. One of the best-known verses in the Bible is John 3:16; "For God so loved the world that he gave his one and only Son, that whosoever believes in him shall not perish but have eternal life. "The word believe isn't just accepting that something may be correct. The word means a faith commitment to the person. Trust, commitment, relationship is the idea. Eternal life is not just life after death. The word carries the idea of quality of life. Real meaning and purpose in life here and now is found in a commitment relationship with God as revealed in Jesus the Christ. Jesus was/is his name. Christ is the New Testament word for Messiah (the anointed) in The Old Testament. No wonder the story of Jesus is so important. He came to give meaning to life, which is love. And he came to give light, direction for living that life.

Part 1
The Birth And Childhood Of Jesus

The Angel's Visit to Zechariah
Luke 1:5-25; 57-80

This is the first of eighty lessons on the life of Jesus. The purpose of the lessons is: to help the reader to know Jesus as her/his Savior and the Savior of the world; to learn through this study of the birth, life, teachings, ministry, death and resurrection of Jesus; and learn and practice how one who follows Jesus is to live. Hopefully the studies will lend help in becoming a good student and reader of the Bible.

We begin our study in the Gospel according to Luke found in the New Testament of the Christian Bible. Luke's story of Jesus begins by saying: many gospels or stories were written about Jesus; he (Luke) did a thorough research; and he noted the period in which the events occurred. Israel was under the dominion of Rome at that time and Herod was the "puppet" king; Luke lets us know Jesus was a Jew. He wrote the story of an event in the life of Zechariah and Elizabeth, and the birth of their son John. As you will see in the second lesson, this connects Jesus with the Jewish history found in the Jewish Bible (the Christian Bible's Old Testament).

During Herod's reign there was a Jewish priest named Zechariah. His wife, Elizabeth, was also from a priestly family. They were a faithful and righteous elderly couple but had no children. It was painful and embarrassing for a Jewish man not to have a son. It was even more painful and embarrassing for Elizabeth because as customary, the wife was said to be barren, the man was not said to be sterile.

This story line is familiar in the Old Testament. Read of Sarah, Abraham's barren wife, in Genesis chapter 18. Jacob and Rachel had the problem (Genesis 30). Read about Samson's mother in Judges chapter 13. See the first chapter of I Samuel for the story of Samuel's mother Hannah. In every story the lesson is that God has power beyond man's power. God is in control.

On an occasion when Zechariah was performing his priestly duty of burning incense at the Temple in Jerusalem, an angel named Gabriel appeared to him. The word angel means messenger and Gabriel means strong man of God. Zechariah was terrified. That is not hard to imagine. Gabriel told him not to be afraid and that next year Elizabeth would bear a son to Zechariah. The son would be named John. He was not to drink strong drink. He would be filled with Holy Spirit and do great things in Israel. That is more than the old man could comprehend or believe. Because of his unbelief Gabriel told Zechariah that he would not be able to speak until the baby was born. This is the power of God at work.

Zechariah and Elizabeth returned from Jerusalem to their home in the hill country. Can you imagine the joy they both experienced when she discovered that she was pregnant? She rejoiced and said her disgrace had been removed. This was the fulfillment of a Jewish wife's dream.

They named the baby John as the angel had instructed. John means God has been gracious. As was Jewish custom, at the appropriate time they took John to the Temple for his circumcision and dedication. When they announced his name as John the people raised questions. Should he not have a family name? They ask Zechariah about the name. He requested and was given a tablet. "His name is John," he wrote.

At that time the voice of Zechariah was restored and like a proud father, he made a speech about his wonderful son. The praise from the lips of Zechariah was inspired by Holy Spirit. It is really a hymn called the Benedictus. Read it in Luke 1:67-79. It tells that John's ministry was to be the "forerunner "for Jesus. John was the one who would introduce Jesus as the long expected Jewish Messiah (the Greek word for Messiah is Christ). Not just his birth, but the life, ministry and death of John are amazing. He is the John we will meet later as John the Baptizer or John the Baptist.

Application to Life

What did this study say to you about God? Does it indicate a love of God for Elizabeth and Zechariah? Does it suggest that God loves you and desires that you trust and love him? Remember this is a study of the life of Jesus who brought the Gospel through his life, death and resurrection. The GOODNEWS is that God loves you, forgives you of your sin and calls you to follow Jesus. Think of what the story may teach about prayer, patience, trust and obedience. Does it teach about parenting?

The Angel's Visit to Mary
Luke 1:26-56

This is the second lesson in a series on the life of Jesus. This lesson is from the Gospel of Luke and relates the appearance of the angel Gabriel to a young Jewish lady named Mary. Recall from lesson one that angel means messenger and Gabriel means strong man of God. So, this is the same angel that appeared to Zechariah telling him that he and his wife, Elizabeth, would have a son. During the story about Zechariah, Elizabeth and John we have the story of the angel Gabriel appearing to Mary.

Can you imagine how startled and afraid Mary must have been? Recall Zechariah, an old man, was "startled and gripped with fear." The angel Gabriel said to her, "Greetings, you who are highly favored! The Lord is with you." (Luke 1:28). She was troubled by the words. But Gabriel said, "Do not be afraid, Mary, you have found favor with God. You will be with child and give birth to a son, and you are to give him the name Jesus. He will be great and will be called the Son of the Highest. The Lord God will give him the throne of his father David, and he will reign over the house of Jacob forever, his kingdom will never end." (Luke 1:30-33). Her first question of how she can, a virgin, have a baby is given an answer. But this is all so mysterious. The message of Gabriel would have been overload for any one. There is so much to say and ask about what Gabriel said that will be discussed throughout the whole study. Right now, note a few of these major themes of Jesus' life and ministry:

The baby was to be named Jesus which means savior or God saves. The name in Hebrew is Joshua. Christ will be his title. It means anointed one. His father David and throne of David are subjects for later lessons. Matthew and Luke trace Jesus' genealogy back to King David and beyond. Matthew traces it back to Abraham and Luke traces it back to Adam. Matthew's emphasis is on Jesus being a Jew in the line of Abraham. Luke infers a universal appeal back to the beginning of creation, son of Adam.

The everlasting reign of Jesus is referred to. Some of the Jewish people were looking for a Messiah (Greek, Christ) to come and deliver them from the Romans and set up an earthly kingdom like that of David. This did not happen and the "kingdom of God" idea will be a major teaching of Jesus.

Move back to the story of Mary. The response of Mary to Gabriel is in verse 38, "I am the Lord's servant. May it be to me as you have said." Would you stop reading for a few moments to think and list the problems Mary may have encountered? Who would not have had a hard time believing how a virgin teenager could be pregnant?

What about Joseph, to whom she was engaged? He could surely break the engagement and bring her before civil court. Were her parents living? What would they do, take her in or throw her out? What about the community, the synagogue, and religious leaders? The list could go on. Who would believe her if she told about seeing an Angel and what he said to her?

Let us see what Mary did. Mary found a safe place. Sometimes it is a good thing to find a quiet place and wise advice. Mary found both. She left Nazareth and went to the hill country to the home of a relative; someone you have already met, Elizabeth. What a meeting. The lady too old to have a baby, but was carrying in her womb, some six months by then, a baby who would be called John. Elizabeth met and greeted the young lady, Mary, who was carrying in her womb the baby who would be named Jesus. Read how Luke recorded this meeting. "When Elizabeth heard Mary's greeting, the baby leaped in her womb, and Elizabeth was filled with the Holy Spirit. In a loud voice she exclaimed 'Blessed are you among women and blessed is the child you shall bear!'" (Luke 1:41-42)

What a relief, joy, comfort Mary must have felt as she heard the accepting greeting and words of understanding from the elder relative. If anyone could understand surely it was Zechariah and Elizabeth. Mary's response to Elizabeth was to break into singing. Read her beautiful hymn in verses 46 -55. It is one of the most beautiful hymns in the Bible. It is called the Magnificat referring to the opening words, "My soul magnifies the Lord." Some translations use the word magnifies instead of glorifies. The hymn praises what God has done and prophesies what kind of Savior Jesus will be. Mary stayed with Elizabeth and Zechariah for three months. Do you think she stayed till John was born?

Application to Life

Have you noticed in these first two studies how God does the unexpected with unlikely persons? Note the elderly and youth are included.

Women and girls are called and used by God in a highly patriarchal society. Who are women in your community and beyond who are being used to better humanity.

What are your own talents, gifts and opportunities? List them. How are you using them? Think of ways you can use them more effectively to help others.

You are called by God to give your life in service to him using your vocation and gifts to bless others.

Joseph, shepherds and wise men did just that as we shall see in our next study on the birth of Jesus.

The Birth of Jesus
Luke 2:1-38; Matthew 1:18-25

"When God is going to do something great, he births a baby." That's a quote from a book written years ago and the baby referred to was Moses. Well, in this lesson on the birth of Jesus, God is about to do something greater. In our previous lesson the angel Gabriel made an appearance to Mary telling her she would be the mother of the baby even though she was a virgin. The lesson discussed some of the problems that Mary might have had to deal with in her family and community. It was noted that she found understanding and comfort from Elizabeth, an aged relative, who would be the mother of John the Baptist.

Now in the birth story of Jesus an angel appeared to Joseph, who is engaged to Mary; a heavenly host appeared to shepherds; and the shepherds go to see the new baby. We are not told how and when Joseph learned that Mary was pregnant. Do you think Mary told him? That would be a good guess. He then was faced with problems. Does he believe her story about Gabriel, the angel talking, to her? What is he to do about the marriage? What about religious and civic duty? Should he expose her to those who would do her harm for being pregnant and not married?

Joseph is in a predicament. Joseph, by the way, is a carpenter. We learn this in Matthew 13:54-56. There it says that some of the locals raised questions about Jesus. They ask if he was not the son of Joseph the carpenter and if his mother was not Mary, the passage goes on to name brothers and sisters.

Guess who showed up? Right, an angel appeared to Joseph. This time the appearance was in a dream. Even in the dream the first words of this angel are, "Do not be afraid ...to take Mary home as your wife, because what is conceived in her is from the Holy Spirit. She will give birth to a son and you shall give him the name Jesus, because he will save his people from their sins."(Matthew 1:20-21) Matthew often referenced Old Testament passages to confirm statements and events. He quoted from Isaiah 7:14 regarding the angel's speech to Joseph. That passage speaks of a young woman (or virgin) who was predicted to have a son. Isaiah was referring to a King who lived at that time. Matthew seems to read it as prophecy. His name was to be Immanuel meaning, God is with us. It is interesting that Matthew ends his book with Jesus' words, "I am with you always, to the very end of the age."

So, Joseph took Mary to be his wife but did not consummate the relationship sexually until after the birth of Jesus. It happened at this time, according to Luke's story, that a census was taken, and every man had to go to his family home town to register. Joseph went to Bethlehem the city of David his ancestor. This was a several days journey south from Nazareth and no doubt difficult for the pregnant Mary. The beautiful story by Luke tells us that they found no room in the inn of the small city but stayed in a shelter for the animals. That night Jesus was born, wrapped warmly and placed in a feeding trough.

What happens when a baby is born? There is celebration. No event like it! Miracle of miracles. A new life has come into the world. Surely, even though far from home and making do in a stable, Mary and Joseph must have given thanks and rejoiced. Were they alone? We are not told, but not far from town, out in the fields, were some shepherds who were dutifully guarding their sheep. They were in for the surprise of their lives. Guess what. An angel showed up. In fact, a "heavenly host" showed up. Surprise! Surprise! They react.

Of course, they were terrified. Guess what the angel said. You got it again. "Do not be afraid." Read the rest of what the angel said, "I bring you good news of great joy which shall be for all the people. Today in the town of David a savior has been born to you; he is Christ the Lord. This will be a sign to you. You will find a baby wrapped in cloths lying in a manger." Luke 2:10-12.

Hardly had the angel finished when the whole sky lit up. There was a whole host of heavenly beings saying, "Glory to God in the highest and on earth peace to men on whom his favor rests." Luke 2:14. As you would think, they took off for Bethlehem at a fast pace to see what had taken place. They found the couple and their new baby, just as the angel had told them. Immediately, they began to tell everyone. Why not? Wouldn't you? They were praising God for the things they had seen and heard.

As was the custom the baby Jesus was taken to the temple in Jerusalem for circumcision, dedication and name giving. This was done on the eighth day after birth. It was at the temple that two other important people spoke about Jesus. One was an old man named Simeon. He praised God with thanks for light that will reach to all people. The other was Anna, an elderly widow who lived in the temple. She praised God with prophetic words about Jesus. Read this in Luke 2: 25-38.

Luke notes that Mary kept all this and "pondered" it in her heart. She no doubt did this over and over as she stayed close to her child, Jesus, throughout his life of teaching, ministry, trial, crucifixion, and resurrection.

Application to Life

Did the angels sing at your birth? Why not? God loves you. Jesus came to show you how much God loves you. Every baby is special and carries the image of God. Did you have a Simeon and /or an Anna; that is, someone who believed in you and was aware of your importance and your gifts; someone who encouraged and helped your parents? Was it a teacher, a friend? an elderly person? Would you be such a person to others? This is what it means to follow Christ. Accept his love and forgiveness. Then love and forgive yourself and others.

Make of list of ways you can be an encourager; a Simeon, an Anna to new parents. Your list may include cards, gifts, prayer, food, chores, keeping other children of the family, taking your turn in the nursery of your church. Make your additions.

The Visit of the Wise Men
Matthew 2:1-12

As noted in an earlier lesson, only Matthew and Luke, of the four Gospels in the New Testament tell us about Jesus' birth and childhood. Both tell about the birth in lesson three, but Matthew adds to his birth story the visit of the magi found in our text listed above. The visit of the wise men or magi happened several months or maybe two years later. This lesson will consist of three sections: The visit of the wise men; the contrasts of Matthew's and Luke's birth stories; the similarities of the two accounts.

It was after the birth of Jesus that the magi or wise men came; looking for one born to be king of the Jews. Who were these men? There is some evidence that they were astrologists. They were following a special star. Maybe they were scholars. They seemed to know history and about the Jews. From their gifts and their long expensive trip, they may have been rich. Where are they from? Arabia, Persia, India who knows? God loved and spoke to them wherever they were. That is a lesson for us. God can speak to whom, when, where and how he wills.

How did they travel? How many were there? Many Christmas pageants have led us to believe there were three because of the three gifts. Usually creches or nativity scenes have camels. Why not horses? The important thing, they were searching for the new king of the Jews. They went to the right place, Jerusalem. Word got to Herod. Herod was a half Jew and puppet king of the Jews appointed by the Roman emperor. He was very jealous of his place. He had killed a wife, a mother in law and two sons. He had prominent citizens arrested and held to be killed at the time of his death so that there would be weeping at that time. This was the man who got his smart men to search and find where a new king was to be born. They found the answer in the book of Micah the prophet. "But you, Bethlehem Ephrathah, though you are small among the clans of Judah, out of you will come for me one who will be ruler over Israel." Micah 5:2.

Herod told the wise men to find this child and come back to tell him, so he could also celebrate his birth. Of course, Herod intended to kill the child. The wise men found the house in Bethlehem where Jesus and his parents lived. They rejoiced and gave their gifts. The gifts were not only generous but significant. Gold is a gift for kings. Incense is a gift for priests to offer in worship. Myrrh is used in preparing bodies for burial. Prophetic gifts? Indeed, they were.

The wise men did not return to Herod but went home another way because they were warned in a dream to do so. Herod intended to kill the child. In fact, when Herod realized that they were not coming back, he ordered that all boys two years old and under in Bethlehem be killed. The two-year limit was based on what the magi had told about the appearing of the star they followed.

Joseph also had a dream, another angel dream. He was told to move his family to Egypt to escape Herod. He did that. Matthew said this happened because an Old Testament passage refers to bringing God's son out of Egypt. That verse of course was referring to Moses, but Matthew is insistent that Jesus is like another Moses.

There are some contrasts between the Matthew and Luke stories of Jesus' birth. Did you ever think of God laughing?

Psalm 2:1-4 in the Old Testament, "Why do nations conspire and the peoples plot in vain? The kings of the earth take their stand and the rulers gather together against the Lord and against his Anointed One". "Let us break their chains," they say, "and throw off their fetters." The one enthroned in heaven **laughs**; the Lord scoffs at them."

Does this remind you a little of Herod's attitude of arrogance and hate? Rulers can think that they are in control, not realizing God has other plans. The Psalms are filled with passages praising the power of God and the futility of man's misused plans and power. So, as we compare the stories of Mathew and Luke there might be some humor, surely irony.

Matthew and Luke have contrasts in their stories: Luke told us that a host of angels appeared to **local shepherds** and sang of Jesus' birth. Mathew told how **foreign magi** saw a new star and found Jesus. See the contrast? Poor shepherds came to an animal shed or cave; not priests to a temple. The magi were men of science and not even Jews.

Contrast the ignored power. You would expect the angels to sing to the priests up at the temple. That is the seat of religious authority. The magi go to the political puppet, Herod, who is afraid even paranoid about his "power." Do you see the serious humor in this? God is in control.

Mathew and Luke have similarities. Both writers have Jesus' birth in Bethlehem, which means house of bread. Jesus will later speak of himself as the bread of life. Both stories are inclusive and universal. The angels in Luke, sang peace on earth and peace among all mankind. The magi in Mathew are foreigners. Jesus came to save all. There was worship and rejoicing by both shepherds and magi.

Application to Life

Reread the stories and find other contrasts and similarities. Do you see any irony? Think about how God loves the rich and poor, the educated and illiterate, people of your race and all other races. What are your thoughts about Jesus being an immigrant? He and his parents went into and came out of Egypt. Egypt received them when their own rulers drove them out. They fled for the safety of their child? Ring any bells today in the USA? What did Paul mean by "Our citizenship (commonwealth) is in heaven" Philippians 3:20? Are we all aliens? What is your response to the stories? Compare it to what the shepherds and magi said and did.

The Childhood of Jesus
Matthew 2:13-23; Luke 2:39-52

The childhood of Jesus lesson picks up where Herod has ordered the boy babies, two years of age and under, in Bethlehem to be killed. Remember from lesson four that Herod is one mean and paranoid man. He was appointed by the emperor of Rome to be a puppet king of the Jews. Herod died in the year 4 B.C. according to historical records. That being so, Jesus was probably born about 6 B.C. Lesson five is divided into three sections: Jesus was taken to Nazareth by way of Egypt; he was taken to Passover in Jerusalem; he grew to be a mature man.

The Bible text for this lesson tells us that after the visit of the magi, God spoke to Joseph in a dream that he should take Mary and baby Jesus and flee to Egypt. This was done in order to avoid Jesus death by Herod. If the trip from Nazareth to Bethlehem seemed long, what about crossing the desert to Egypt. The story does not tell how this was accomplished. Do you think they were able to find a caravan? Surely a couple with a young child would not attempt it alone. Matthew inserts one of his Old Testament quotes here about God bringing his son out of Egypt. The text had to do with the Jews escaping from Egypt led by Moses.

They stayed in Egypt till the death of Herod. Then they decided to go home to Nazareth. So, Jesus' growing up years and until he was about thirty were spent in Nazareth. Jesus probably had wonderful Jewish teaching from Joseph and Mary. He would have also learned the Hebrew Scripture at his local synagogue. Would you not think that he was taught the wood working trade of Joseph? As the oldest child, he assumed a great deal of responsibility for care of the family. Many believe Joseph died during Jesus' growing up years. The reasoning is since Joseph, so prominent until Jesus is twelve, is not mentioned again. This brings us to the next section.

Luke tells us that when Jesus was about twelve Joseph and Mary took him to the Passover festival in Jerusalem. This seems to have been a yearly trip for Joseph. The Passover was and is an extremely important event in the life of Jewish people. Its celebrated God's deliverance of the Jewish people from Egyptian bondage. You can read about this in the Book of Exodus.

It may have been at this time that Jesus had his Bar Mitzvah. Which means "son of the commandment." A ceremony when a thirteen-year-old boy was declared a man. That is, he was old enough to understand and obey the commandments. Think about this as the story continues. By the way, girls have their Bat Mitzvah at age twelve.

When the festival was over Joseph and Mary started home, probably with the caravan they came with. It was dangerous to travel alone. At evening camp time, Jesus was nowhere to be found. Sound sort of like teenagers? Joseph and Mary returned to Jerusalem and found Jesus, on the third day, in the Temple. He was asking questions and listening to the discussion by the religious leaders. They were stunned by his knowledge and wisdom.

Mary was somewhat exasperated. Wonder why, wouldn't you be? "Son, why have you treated us like this? " Luke 2:48. Jesus answered: "Why were you searching for me? Didn't you know I had to be in my Father's house?" Students of the Bible spend a lot of time discussing reasons this could have happened. Do not ascribe to him the attribute of knowing everything at age twelve or thirteen. Let him grow, learn, change. He is a human being. Here are two reasons to think about. You don't have known everything.

What if Jesus had been told the story of Samuel (see I Samuel chapters 1 & 2 in The Old Testament). Hannah had prayed for a child. God heard. She had a son and named him Samuel (God hears). She promised God if she had a son, she would give him back to the Lord. When he was weaned, she brought him to the tabernacle (place of worship before the temple) and LEFT HIM with Eli the priest. She came yearly to visit and bring him clothes She sang a hymn very similar to the Magnificat of Mary. Is it possible that Jesus felt he was supposed to stay? Parents and teens are still known to have miscommunications.

2. Jesus spoke to Mary about necessity of him being in HIS FATHER'S house. Some Bible translations say his Father's business.

Father may be the key word here. Is Jesus becoming aware that his Father, God, takes preeminence over his father Joseph? Later in the Gospels when Jesus was being criticized his family went to take him home. See Matthew 12:46-50. Verse fifty Jesus says, "For whoever does the will of my Father in heaven is my brother and sister and mother."

Whatever you conclude, note what Luke 2:51 says, "Then he went down to Nazareth and was obedient to them." Was he ever. Apparently, he remained with the family until about 30 as we shall see in the next lesson. This has to say something important about what Jesus' family meant to him. He did his duty as the eldest child. His mother never forgets. And he never forgot his Mother.

"And Jesus grew in wisdom and stature and in favor with God and men." (Luke 2:52) In this section take the following statement and discuss or think through its meaning. **Grow toward maturity in your total person in your total relationships.** Do you think it says something like Jesus' growth? Take the sentence apart. **Grow**. You could use change, develop, learn (no change, no learning) or other synonym. **Toward.** Not to, but toward, you never get there. It is a lifelong process. **Maturity.** Becoming all you can or was intended to be. Becoming the real you. **Total Person.** Mental, physical, emotional, social, psychological, spiritual, what else? **Total Relationships.** Relationship to self, God, family, others, things, nature, What else?

Application to Life

Was Jesus saying all other relationships for him were determined by his relationship to God? Considering verse 52, what should be your response? Does following Jesus mean the same thing as putting God first in your life? Take time to examine your life by the definition of maturity given above. Discuss the definition if you are in a group study. The next session is on Jesus' Baptism and Temptation.

Part 2

The Beginning Of Jesus' Ministry

The Baptism and Temptations of Jesus
Matthew 3:1-17; 4:1-11; Mark 1:1-13; Luke 3:1-38; 4:1-13; John 1:19-34

This lesson jumps about seventeen years in time from the last lesson. There Jesus was about thirteen years old and the next we know about him is from the passages of this lesson. According to Luke3:23, "Now Jesus was about thirty years old, when he began his ministry." All four gospels are used in this lesson. Each tells about the baptism of Jesus and all, but John tell about the temptations event. This lesson will take the two events in order and then suggest some life applications.

John is referred to in the passages as the one who baptized Jesus. This John is the son of Elizabeth and Zechariah. Recall their story from Part 1, lesson 1. The scripture was Luke 1:5-25; 57-80. John would have been expected to be a priest like his father. But, surprise! John shows up in the wilderness of the Jordan River, not at the temple in Jerusalem. What is going on? Look at the contrasts: a river, not the temple; a wilderness not Jerusalem; camel hair coat, not priestly vestments; not fine cuts of meat from the sacrifices, but locusts and wild honey. Do you think of other surprises?

Listen to his message. Matthew 3:1-2, "In those days John the Baptist came preaching in the wilderness of Judea and saying, 'Repent, for the kingdom of heaven has come near.'" There are two terms to study here. What is the meaning of repent and what is the kingdom of heaven. Mark and Luke called it kingdom of God. It is thought that, Matthew, writing to a Jewish Christian congregation, used heaven because the word God was so scared the faithful Jews would not say it.

Repent means to change your mind, heart and direction. Change the way you treat others. Read Luke's answer when some asked, "What shall we do?"

The kingdom of God means the rule or reign of God. John said it had come or was near at hand. What does the kingdom look like? Quaker Christians have what they call testimonies. They are individual and community virtues. I found this in Philip Gulley's book, *Living the Quaker Way*, He is one of my favorite authors.

The first letter of each virtue spells **SPICE**. Use this to discuss how SPICE is like the message of John.

S is for SIMPLICITY. Know the difference between needs and wants. Avoid greed.

P is for PEACE. Jesus would become the model for nonviolent protest.

I is for INTEGRITY. This is wholeness, akin to salvation. Being real, honest, humble.

C is for COMMUNITY. Think of the common good. You are not independent.

E is for EQUALITY. Though we are each unique, diverse, different in many ways, we are each and all created in the image of God. Discuss this.

What is baptism? Baptism is a symbolic act depicting repentance, change. The word means to immerse. It symbolizes the burial to an old life and resurrection to a new life.

Why was Jesus baptized you may ask if he did not need to change his way of living?

Good question. Think about it. Is Jesus saying by his action that he agreed with what John was doing and preaching? Was Jesus expressing his real humanity?

Was he identifying with the human condition? Was Jesus enacting his future burial and resurrection Jesus retreated to a wilderness place. Do you think the retreat may have been for prayer, fasting and determining the direction and purpose of his ministry? The nature of the temptations seems to suggest that. Only Matthew and Luke list the temptations. The first was to turn stones into bread to satisfy his personal hunger. He had fasted for forty days and was famished. Could this temptation to make his ministry one of possessions?

There are natural hungers and needs of human beings that need to be met. But selfish greed can lead to a multitude of wrongs. Physical possessions are not enough to satisfy the spiritual needs as Jesus so clearly points out in the answer he provides. Was he saying that his ministry was more than feeding the physical. His concern was the whole person.

Next temptation is to do the spectacular. Jump off the steeple of the temple to the valley below. God will save you. Note the Adversary can quote scripture. Jesus knows this is testing, tempting God and says as he refuses this route to fame and prestige. His was a way of love relationship, not to gain a following by doing something useless and spectacular.

Jesus is shown the kingdoms of the world. If he will bow down and worship Satan, they would belong to him. Is this the power crave? Jesus refused, knowing that the power of Satan's way is wrong. You may want to put other names beside possessions, prestige and the power of war and violence. How do these temptations relate to what John told those who asked what they should do, or how they should repent? How do the temptations relate to the Quaker S.P.I.C.E?

Angels came and ministered to Jesus. He was filled with the Spirit of God and ready to begin his ministry.

Application to Life

What is the meaning of baptism to you?

Go back through this lesson and ask yourself or discuss in a group the questions found in each section.

What temptations do you have? Do you find help from Jesus' words to resist?

How do the SPICE words relate to repentance for you?

Do you think repentance is a daily need or once for all?

Jesus Called His First Disciples
John 1:35-51

This lesson connects Jesus baptism by John to the beginning of Jesus' ministry. There is a shift from John the Baptist's ministry to the ministry of Jesus. John had said that Jesus would increase and he (John) would decrease. He had a great spirit. To avoid confusion, a distinction needs to be made between John the Baptist and John, the author of the Gospel of John. We will learn more about the author John later.

The word disciple needs some explanation. It comes from the word discipline. It is used to refer to a learner or student. Teachers had disciples who stayed with and followed them to learn their teaching and way of life.

This lesson will divide the Bible passage into three parts: Jesus called disciples to participate; participating disciples called others; and participating disciples were seekers.

The setting for this lesson has John with two of his disciples and they saw Jesus passing by. John said, "Look, the Lamb of God." (1:36)

The two disciples leave John and follow Jesus. Were they timid, showing respect or in awe of Jesus? He stopped and asked them what they wanted. Jesus takes the initiative. That is his way. Their answer was to ask where he was staying. Was that really what they wanted to know or were they taken by surprise at Jesus interest in them?

Whatever the motive they had, they got the right answer from Jesus. "Come and See. "They were about to learn more than where he was staying. That is what discipleship is about, "come and see." Participate.

Andrew was one of the disciples and the other is unnamed. They spend the remainder of the day with Jesus. What would you guess Jesus taught them? It may well have been about the Kingdom of God. The Kingdom of God was a major topic of Jesus' teaching.

Andrew was convinced that Jesus was the hoped-for Messiah. Messiah means anointed one. Anointed, as to become a king. Most who expected a Messiah had in mind a military king. Jesus was not that kind of messiah.

Participating disciples live and speak that others will desire to follow Jesus.

Andrew went to find his brother Simon. When he found him, John 1:41-42 says that he told Simon "We have found the Messiah (that is, the Christ)" And he brought him to Jesus. Jesus looked at him and acknowledged that his name was Simon, but Jesus gave him another name. He called him Cephas (Aramaic) or Peter (Greek). Both words mean rock. Peter was to become a leading disciple, but Andrew is only mentioned a couple more times by name in the gospels. But in both places, he was bringing persons to Jesus. Read these in John 6:8,9 and 12:22.

The lesson text says Jesus also called Philip. He said to him, "Follow me."1:43. Philip found Nathanael. The text, 1:45-46, says, "We have found the one Moses wrote about in the Law, and about whom the prophets also wrote, Jesus of Nazareth the son of Joseph." "Nazareth! Can anything good come from there?" Nathanael asked. "Come and see," said Philip. This leads to the next idea. Jesus words, "Come and see" and "Come and follow me" are excellent descriptions of what it means to be a disciple of Jesus both then and now. Come see, learn, and participate.

Participating disciples should not fear, but feel free to ask questions. That is the way to learn. Nathanael questioned that anything good could come from Nazareth. Did that come from a town rivalry between Bethsaida and Nazareth? Was it a 'put down' about the size of Nazareth? What is important here is that Nathanael was open enough and comfortable to ask questions. Jesus surprised him when he told Andrew of seeing him under a fig tree and knew he was a man of no guile. That got his attention quickly. He was so taken by Jesus that he said, verse 49, "Rabbi, you are the Son of God; you are the king of Israel." When Jesus said he saw him under a fig tree, he could be noting a place of peace. Sitting under the tree may refer to a peaceful place of meditation. Could it be a prophetic?

picture of peace to come. The prophets spoke of a time when all would have such peace.

You can feel comfortable to ask questions about Jesus, God, the Bible, meaning of life and other of life's doubts and puzzles. God knows your heart. He loves you. He invites you to come and see. Come and follow.

Application to Life

The words of Jesus, "Follow me," are your invitation to commit your life to him, to learn from him and to live your life by his teachings. The Good News is that God loves you, has forgiven you and wants you to accept his love and forgiveness. God's Spirit will help you to grow toward maturity. The idea of "follow me" carries the meaning of repentance. You must turn, change directions when you follow Jesus.

If you are a follower of Jesus, you will want to tell others, "come and see."

Tell them what he means to you. List questions that you have about what you believe and what you have been taught. You may doubt or have questions about what the Bible says and how it applies to life in this day and society. Ask, Seek, Study, Be Open,

Jesus Performed His First Miracle
John 2:1-12

The previous lesson was John's version of Jesus calling his first disciples. John used a lot of symbolic language; metaphors, symbols, words that carry two or more meanings. He used the word sign instead of miracle for Jesus miraculous deeds. Signs point the direction to something else.

In this lesson think about: Jesus enjoyed parties; Jesus turned water into wine; and Jesus made wine a symbol of abundant joy and grace.

Jesus first sign according to John's story takes place at a wedding. The wine was all gone. He turned water into wine. Does it seem strange to you that Jesus turned water to wine and/or that Jesus enjoyed parties? More than a dozen Gospel stories tell of Jesus eating with persons. He ate with "good folk" and with those considered "bad guys" or "sinners." He ate with friend and foe. He ate with male and female. He ate with one or a few and he ate with crowds. He ate where invited or just showed up. He also told many eating and drinking stories. Room prohibits telling the stories here, but here is a list that you might read in your personal study or discuss in your group.

When Jesus healed Peter's mother in law she got up and served them. Mark 1:29-39. Matthew gave a banquet for Jesus and invited his friends. Matthew 9:9-17

He ate with Pharisees. Luke 14:1-35

He ate with Zacchaeus a tax collector. Luke 19:1-29

He fed 5,000. Matthew 14:13-21.

He ate with his disciples on the night before his death. John 13-17.

He ate with a couple on the Emmaus road. Luke 24:13-35

He ate with the disciples on the night of his resurrection. Luke 24:36-43.

He ate with the disciples on the sea shore. John 21:1-14

You may want to read some of Jesus' stories that include eating. For example, the stories in Luke: 15:11-52; 14:7-14, 15-24; Luke 16:19-31.

Wine for the Jews was a symbol of JOY. Weddings were festive occasions. They go together. The invited guests were there to celebrate. Though drinking to excess was frowned upon, wine drinking was a custom and a joyful one.

Mary, Jesus mother, may have had some responsibility in the wedding. It is Mary who told Jesus that the wine was gone. Jesus made a reply that may sound harsh. But that isn't consistent with his nature. Does it remind you of a conversation they had in lesson five? Jesus was left behind in Jerusalem and Mary and Joseph must return. They found him in the temple. Mary was somewhat upset, and Jesus seemed surprised that she did not know that he would be in the temple. In this lesson, Jesus seemed to show indifference, but Mary knew better. Don't you think she knew Jesus would do something to help? Mary had done what she could, she told Jesus. She told the servants to "Do what he (Jesus) tells you." Then she waited.

You have read the text for the lesson. There were six empty water pots. Each had a 20 gallon or more capacity. The water that had been in the pots was used for washing guests' dust covered feet and for ceremonially washing the guest's hands. Jesus told the servants to fill the pots with water. Now there was 120 plus gallons of water. Then Jesus told them to serve the one in charge. That was done and the one in charge asked why the best wine was saved until last. Custom called for the good first and late in the festivities, if necessary, serve the cheaper wine. One hundred twenty gallons of water was turned to one hundred twenty plus gallons of the finest wine!!!

Some think that wine is a symbol of Holy Spirit. The occasion would suggest the symbol of Joy. But whichever you choose the lesson is the same. Jesus' Joy or Holy Spirit is abundant. There is enough for everyone. This is a theme to look for in future lessons. God's love, grace, mercy, forgiveness, joy is extravagant!!! They know no end. They are for all.

In Jesus' address to the disciples, on the night before he was crucified, he told them, "I have told you this so that my joy may be in you and that your joy may be complete." John 15:11. In First John 1:4 near the end of the New Testament, John said, "We write this to make your joy complete." The joy of wedding love is a New Testament symbol for Christ and his church.

Application to Life

For your thought and/or group discussion

1. Do you think followers of Jesus should be joyful? Why/why not?
2. Discuss how sign and miracle may be the same or different.
3. How could this story help you relate to weddings and other family events?
4. Relate the abundance of wine (joy, grace) to life application.
5. Can you have joy during trouble? Why? How?
6. Discuss how marriage and commitment are like "believing in Jesus."

Jesus Cleansed the Temple
John 2:13-22

Have you ever thought of Jesus getting angry? Some think the text for this lesson strongly implies that he did. Certainly, he had reason to be angry. But think of other feelings he could have had and discuss or think why: disappointment; frustration; disapproval; shame; sadness. You may think of other feelings.

Try to imagine yourself in Jesus' place, in the priest's job, in the place of the worshippers and the sellers. There must have been a multitude of opinions and emotions before and after Jesus "cleansed" the temple. How did the noise of the crowd and animals affect them? What about the buying, selling and exchanging?

This lesson has three questions: What did Jesus do? When did the event occur? Why did Jesus "cleanse" the temple?

What did Jesus do that is called cleansing the temple? The annual Passover feast and celebration was in Jerusalem. The Passover celebrated the exodus of the Jews from Egyptian slavery. Thousands of Jews from far and near were in Jerusalem. They came to pay a required temple tax with Jewish tax coins. They came to do animal sacrifice of lambs as done on the night of the exodus. So, there were money exchangers at the temple. National coins would need to be exchanged for Jewish coins. A profitable charge was made for the exchange. Many worshippers would need to buy the proper and inspected animal for sacrifice. Thus, within the court of the Gentiles (anyone not a Jew) all the buying, selling, exchanging and collecting were going on.

The text does not say that Jesus was angry, but that he made a whip of cords and drove out the sellers and animals and overturned the tables of the exchangers. Verse 16 says that Jesus said to the dove sellers, "Get these out of here! Stop turning my Father's house into a market."

When did Jesus do this? When in the chronology of the ministry of Jesus did this cleansing of the temple take place? All four Gospels (Matthew, Mark, Luke, and John) tell of the event. John places the even near the beginning of Jesus' ministry but the other three writers put the story during the week of Jesus 'crucifixion, near the end of their accounts. Why the difference? Were there two such events? Some think so, others believe it to be very unlikely. The reason being that this event was high on the list of accusations that got Jesus killed. Suggestion to consider. Have you ever read the last chapter of a novel early in order to see how it ends?

Could John have done something similar here? He could be making a prophetic statement near the beginning of his book. He is setting the stage for the counter cultural and counter false religion of Jesus' ministry.

Why do you think Jesus did this cleansing of the temple? Was it also a sign? Verse 18, The Jews then responded to him, "What sign can you show us to prove your authority to do all this?" Be careful that you do not think of all Jews when John uses the term. He does this often. He is referring some religious power players who opposed Jesus. Remember, Jesus was a Jew. John's use of the word has caused racial bias in some readers. The answer Jesus gave is in verse 19, "Destroy this temple and I will raise it in three days." The original temple was built by King Solomon the son of Kings David. Read about its elaborate building and dedication in First Kings chapters five through nine and Second Chronicles chapters three through seven in the Old Testament. It was destroyed by the Babylonians about the year 586 B.C. It was rebuilt and dedicated between by about 515 -521 B.C.E. had been worked on and embellished by Herod for some forty-six years at the time of Jesus' ministry. It would be destroyed by the Romans in 70 A.D.

Jesus' prediction of destruction of the temple has two meanings. The building would be destroyed. But John makes it clear that Jesus is predicting his death and resurrection. Verse 19, Jesus answered them, "Destroy this temple and I will raise it again in three days." Verse 20-21, They replied, "It has taken forty-six years to build this temple and you are going to raise it in three days?" But the temple he had spoken of was his body. Was Jesus saying he was the new temple, where God meets people? Not just Jews, but all people. The temple was to be a house of prayer for **all nations**.

Application to Life

Does this story give warning to Christian persons, churches, organizations, denominations, etc. of the danger of misused power? What does "house of prayer for all nations" say to you about everyone should be welcomed at your place of worship?

In an upcoming lesson Jesus will say that God is Spirit and they who worship him must do so in spirit and truth. Is your church open to all people? Does this story have anything to say about the value of persons versus buildings? Religion, Christian included, has a bad history of seeking to violently control people. Threat, violence, coercion is not Jesus way. Love is his way.

Jesus Met with Nicodemus
John 2:23-25; 3:1-21

John 2:23-25 sets the stage for the study of Jesus' meeting with Nicodemus. Jesus was in Jerusalem again and had caused quite a stir among the people with his teachings and signs. Though John chose only a few of Jesus' signs for his Gospel, it is evident that Jesus did many more. In fact, the last verse in his book says, "Jesus did many other things as well. If every one of them were written down, I suppose that even the whole world would not have room for the books that would be written."

The story of Nicodemus is one of the best-known stories in the New Testament. Remember John uses signs and symbols and they often have two meanings: physical and spiritual; surface and depth; obvious and hidden. Examples are: in chapter one: Word means wisdom and incarnation (v.14 The Word became flesh); in chapter 2, wine is drink and joy; in chapter 3, new birth or born again, physical and spiritual.

Three sections to guide our thinking in this lesson are: Jesus had a conversation with Nicodemus; Jesus' symbolic terms; and Jesus came to save the world.

Nicodemus was a Pharisee. The Pharisees were a Jewish religious sect that was very devoted to keeping all 613 laws and traditions of their religion. An earlier study said the word Jews can be misleading in John's book. So, can Pharisee. Some of them were very opposed to Jesus. That does not mean that they all were out to get him. It is dangerous to classify all persons in a group in the same way.

Nicodemus was a ruler or "a member of the Jewish ruling council" (3:1). This probably meant the Sanhedrin, the supreme court of the Jews, both civil and religious. Why do you think he came at night to see Jesus? Was its fear of being seen with Jesus? Did he simply want privacy? Did he come to warn Jesus?

He began the conversation by highly complementing Jesus. He gave him the title Rabbi. Who is the "we" in verse two? Whoever, they are convinced that Jesus is from God or he could not do the wonderful works. Do you think Nicodemus was sincere and truthful?

Jesus disregarded his words and instead of answering or asking a question, Jesus made a statement, "Very truly I tell you, no one can see the kingdom of God, unless they are born again" (v.3). Nicodemus asks how an adult can be born again. No way can he reenter his mother's body and be born again. Here are those two meanings again.

Find words in the Bible passage that need explanation. Make a list.

Here are a few of the terms you may have on your list.

Born again is one of many biblical terms used to describe conversion or salvation. You have read how Nicodemus misunderstood the term. Would you have understood? Could it be like repentance, a complete change of mind, heart and direction? Matthew 18:2&3: He (Jesus) called a little child to him and placed the child among them (his disciples). And he said, "Truly I tell you, unless you change and become like little children, you will never enter the kingdom of heaven." See I Corinthians 3:1,2; Hebrews 5:12-14; I Peter1:3.

Kingdom of God or heaven is described in the Model Prayer that Jesus taught his disciples. Matthew 6:9,10, "Our Father in heaven, hallowed be your name**, your kingdom come, your will be done, on earth as it is in heaven."**

Perish could be to die, lost as wandering from the right way. Many would say this means hell, eternal punishment. It does not say that. More like missing the potential in life and thus **condemning** or judging oneself as having failed to live the truth.

Verse 16 may be the best-known verse in the New Testament. This is the Good News. God loved the world everyone and everything he created so much he gave his Son (birth, life, teachings, death and resurrection) to reveal that love in flesh. Anyone who wants the Jesus kind of life must commit to follow his way. Not to do so is to miss the meaning of life. Love is the way of the life of Jesus. Warning! Be careful not to think that Jesus died to appease an angry and vengeful God. It was the loving God's idea to save a wayward world through living life and defeating death to show the world what the loving God is like. His desire is for you to follow Jesus and know the good and lasting life. It begins here, now, not just after death.

Application to Life

Do word study to find how the words needing explanation are used in other places in the New Testament. Follow Jesus' commands. Those are to love God with your whole being and love others as you love yourself.

Jesus Met the Samaritan Woman
John 3:22-36; 4:1-42

The wonderful spirit of John the Baptist is shown in John 3:22-36. Following the conversation with Nicodemus, Jesus and his disciples remained in Judea, preaching and baptizing. Some of John's disciples were having some trouble adjusting to the fact that Jesus was having more followers than John. But John knew and was happy about that. He reminded them that he was not the Christ, but had come to point the way to Jesus, the Christ. Jesus heard that the Pharisees knew about all this and decided it was time to go back to Galilee. Jesus knew the thinking of the religious leaders and that rather than confront them so early in his ministry, he must go back to Galilee. He had so much to do and in limited time.

This lesson has a large scripture passage so there will be four sections: Jesus had to go through Samaria; Jesus met a woman at the well and gave the woman living water; The woman became a missionary for Jesus. Why did John write that Jesus **had to go through Samaria?** Jews normally crossed the Jordan River and traveled on the east side of it to avoid going through Samaria. Judea was in the south and Galilee and Sea of Galilee were far north. In between was Samaria. All were bordered on the east by the Jordan River and on the west by the Mediterranean Sea.

There was great racial and religious prejudice between Jews and Samaritans. The united Israel (all 12 tribes) was ruled by King David and then his son King Solomon. The territory included what in Jesus time was called Judea, Samaria and Galilee. When Solomon died the kingdom was divided. Read this in I Kings 12 and the chapters following.

In 722 B.C. the ten tribes in the north called Israel were conquered and taken into exile by Assyria. This territory included what was later called Samaria. Only the weak and poor were left behind. Captives from other conquered lands were moved in by Assyria. These two groups intermarried and came to be called Samaritans. This was sinful to Jews in Judah (the southern kingdom) to marry outside the race and religion. Many of these "half breeds" and Jews hated each other. So 'through Samaria' was not the normal route?

Jesus met a Samaritan woman at a well near Sychar. Wells were good places to meet. Read about other men who met women at wells in Genesis 24, Abraham's servant; 29, Jacob; and Exodus 2, Moses. Jesus and his disciples had a long morning walk, they got to the well near the town of Sychar about noon. The disciples were hungry and went into town to buy food. Jesus was tired and rested by the well. Jesus was human, he did get tired and thirsty. A woman came to draw water. This may indicate that she felt ostracized from other women and came alone in the heat of the day.

Jesus initiates a conversation with her by asking for a drink of water. He then takes the water as a metaphor for that which gives permanent relief from thirst. As in previous lessons from John, we have double meaning. The woman was thinking literal water, Jesus is referring to a relationship of love with God. Water can satisfy physical thirst, but only God satisfies the thirst for God. She did not understand. Jesus is patient. He told her to go and bring her husband.

You can feel the tension strike. Jesus caused her to look at herself. She had married five times was living with a man to whom she was not married. Do not be quick to judge her. A man could divorce a wife for the most trivial reasons. She did not have the same right. Work was not easy to find for women in that society. Marriage was almost a ticket for survival.

She changed the subject saying Jesus must be a prophet to know so much about her. How did Jesus know about her? Good question. She continued the religious talk about the place of worship for Samaritans was this mount, but Jews worshiped in Jerusalem. Jesus gave one of his most prophetic statements to the woman. Verse 24, "God is spirit, and his worshipers must worship him in Spirit and in truth" She thinks he is the Messiah and Jesus said "I am."

How much did she understand? Whatever, she left her water bucket and ran to town to tell the men (who were they?) about Jesus. He must be the Messiah. Verse 28, "Come, see...." Remember reading those words earlier. They went, saw and heard and trusted. So much more to the story, read and reread it. Discuss it and seek application to life.

Application to Life

List the barriers Jesus broke in talking with this woman…race, religion, etc.

List the barriers or prejudices in your life toward other people: race, religion, nationality, skin color, social, economic, where one lives, what one wears, what one drives, how one sounds, and where one goes. Fill up the page or board. Why do you have these feeling, where did they come from? What can you do to treat and feel toward others like you think Jesus would have you feel and think? You may begin by not classifying people.

Part 3

Jesus' Great Galilean Ministry

Jesus Healed the Nobleman's Son
Matthew 4:17; Mark 1:14-15
Luke 4:14-15; John 4:46-54

This is the first of twenty-four lessons in a series on Jesus' Galilean ministry. Half of these stories deal with healings by Jesus. The Synoptic Gospels (Matthew, Luke and Mark) passages simply identify time and place. Only John tells the story for this study. Though in Galilee, instead of Judea, it is of interest to look back at the variety of people Jesus encountered. This trend will continue. Remember John the Baptist, Andrew, Peter Philip, Nathaniel, the wedding workers, Nicodemus, the sellers, traders, priests, Pharisees, the Samaritan woman and men. And now, a "nobleman" visited him. Jesus had returned to Cana in Galilee; where he turned water into wine (Part 2, lesson 3). The people welcomed him because they had seen what he had done in Jerusalem.

A new story begins with the last sentence in verse 46: "And there was a certain royal official whose son lay sick at Capernaum." In this short story a child broke down barriers; a child was healed and a whole household was changed. Watch for JOY again like in John 2.

The previous lesson Jesus Met the Samaritan Woman, all kinds of relationship barriers came tumbling down. Jesus had a habit of walking right through things that keep people from each other and recognizing God's love. In this story as a sick child opens the way. Who the nobleman was is not told. The word is translated in the New International Version of the Bible "royal official." It means a courtier of or advisor to or in the presence of a king. He lived in Capernaum of Galilee. Herod (not the one in Part 1 lesson 4) was Rome's puppet king of Galilee. The nobleman probably had wealth and political power. But his child, his son, was sick, near death. Few things are as fearful, frustrating, even devastating to good parents as a sick child. The age of the child is not given, but it was a son. Sorry, but in the patriarchal society boy babies seem more important. A point for your thought and your study group to discuss.

Now, to barriers and their removal. Contrast this politically, socially, economically, or other ways. The **nobleman:** wealthy, in the king's court, praised as a public figure, etc. from the important trade and military city, Capernaum. The Romans had a military "base" there. **Jesus:** poor, carpenter, itinerant preacher, from Nazareth.

Read the text. Does Jesus answer to the nobleman's request surprise you? Verse 48: "unless you people see signs and wonders," Jesus told him, "you will never believe." Was Jesus letting the man know that he (Jesus) knew the man would not have come except as a last resort? Could Jesus have been making known the positions, wealth, titles, statuses. did not influence him? But the fact that the man and the child were human beings in need elicited Jesus' compassion. Listen for the heart-rending plea of the man in verse 49: "Sir, come down before my child dies. "Verse 50: "Go," Jesus replied, "your son will live."

As the man went home, he was met by a servant with the good news that his son was living. He inquired about the time of change in the son's condition. The servant told him the hour the son began to improve. It was the same time that Jesus had told him that his son would live. Can you imagine the joy and thanksgiving that flooded his heart? The story says that the man and his whole household believed. That was a turning. Jesus was the Messiah. No way for us to know what all believe meant to this man, his family members and servants, but they were changed from grief to joy, from gloom to thanksgiving. Do you think they put trust in Jesus that led them to follow his teaching?

Verse 54: "This was the second sign Jesus performed after coming from Judea to Galilee. Continue to watch for signs and "I am" sayings in John's Gospel.

Application to Life

Discuss with your group or think about the importance of children to Jesus. For help see: Matthew 18:1-14; Mark 10:13-16; Luke 18:15-17. Think about ways children help adults break down barriers. Also discuss how children are taught to fear or hate others.

What did you see in this story that you need to give further thought and prayer to? The next lesson is Jesus Rejected at Nazareth, read Matthew 4:13-16 and Luke 4:16-31.

Jesus Rejected at Nazareth
Matthew 4:13-16; Luke 4:16-31

Matthew did not give the Nazareth synagogue story, so this lesson will focus on the Luke passage. Reminder: it is improbable to have an exact chronological blending of the four Gospel stories of Jesus. Remember, each of the four writers wrote at different times, to different readers or churches and with varied emphases. John had Jesus in Jerusalem in most of his book, while the other three writers give a great emphasis to the Galilean ministry. They all four gave nearly half of their space to the days before the crucifixion of Jesus and after his resurrection. These variations should enrich the study, not cause a problem. The event in this study makes two divisions: Jesus read and interpreted Scripture, and Jesus was praised and then rejected. The event is very important for a sound interpretation of Jesus. It should help understand who he is and what he came to do.

Jesus had come home to Nazareth in Galilee. As was his habit, he attended the synagogue meeting on the Sabbath. Reminder: there was one Temple. It was in Jerusalem. It was for worship through animal, grain, etc. sacrifice carried out by priests. There was a synagogue, gathering place in most towns. It was for worship through prayer, singing, reading and discussion of Scripture. Meetings were led by lay persons. Thus, Jesus was asked to read the scripture lesson. He was given the scroll of Isaiah. He found the place which in current Bibles would be chapters 58 and 61. He stood to read and sat to teach or interpret as was the custom.

At this point, read Isaiah 58:6 and 61:1-2. There you find what Luke said Jesus read. It would be well to read the entire chapters to get a better contrast of the justice God expected and the injustice that was occurring: when Isaiah wrote; when Jesus read; and present day as you read. Do you think Jesus read more than Luke quoted?

After reading, Jesus sat. Luke 4:21, He began by saying to them, "Today this scripture is fulfilled in your hearing." Is Jesus saying, "I am the Messiah?"

They were expecting a King like David to destroy Rome. But these passages talk about doing justice, setting free captives, taking care of the poor. Noted in an earlier lesson, the Kingdom of God, the reign of God, means "Thy will be done on earth as it is in heaven. "The following lessons may give insight to this. Looking ahead, Jesus will set all kinds of people free. Some are bound by disease and he heals. He pays special attention to the poor, the out casts and marginalized, those who have eyes, but can't see and those who are physically blind. He touches the untouchables. He is especially kind to women and children. All that he did he summarized: "So then in everything, do to others what you would have them do to you, for this sums up the Law and the Prophets" Matthew 7:12.

Confused or not they praised the home town speaker whom they think is a son of Joseph. Jesus knew himself to be a prophet. A prophet can see what is and tell where it is leading. Jesus knew the prophets were often killed for telling the truth which conflicted with religious and/or political power. Even knowing this Jesus continued to illustrate his point with stories about Elijah and his disciple Elisha.

You may like to read the stories in I Kings 17:8-16; and II Kings 5:11-17. Elijah, helped a poor widow in Sidon and through Elisha, God healed a Syrian general. How quickly emotions can change! The folk in the synagogue in a moment of time changed from cheering and praising to crying out in rage. They changed because Jesus was saying that God cared for the enemy. Be very careful when your religion becomes exclusive. God loves all people. They went from claps to slaps. They wanted to hurl him over the cliff. Jesus made a quick exit to save his life. He moved to Capernaum. Prejudice was a major problem then and is now, no matter where you live.

Application to Life

Life is all about relationships. Try the following activity to improve relationships. Down the center of a page write RELATIONSHIP. To the left of each letter write words, beginning with that letter, that hinder good relationships. To the right of each write words, beginning with that letter that enhance good relationships. Discuss each.

Jesus Called Four Disciples
Matthew 4:18-22; Mark 1:16-20; Luke 5:1-11

Prophets in the Old Testament had disciples. Remember Elijah and Elisha in the last lesson? Elisha was a disciple of Elijah. Greek philosophers had disciples. Pharisees had disciples. John the Baptist had disciples, remember? John 1:35-51. This lesson is about Jesus calling four disciples to follow him.

A disciple is a learner, a student. A disciple is taught by listening to and observing the teacher. He learns by being with the teacher and practicing his/her teaching. She/he learns by obeying the teacher. Matthew chapter ten is an example of Jesus instructing his disciples. "A disciple is not above his teacher….it is enough for the disciple to be like the teacher" verses 24-25. The word disciple is used more than 250 times in the New Testament.

Matthew copies Mark's account almost to a word. Luke, as in the previous lesson, adds a story. Keep Mark and Matthew in mind while following Luke's story. Jesus gave four professional fishermen a lesson for life and called them to follow him. The four were James and his brother John and Simon and his brother Andrew. Recall meeting Andrew, a disciple of John the Baptist, and Simon, whom Jesus called Cephas or Peter meaning rock (John 1:35-51)?

There does not have to be a problem with the differences in Luke's, Mark's and Matthew's account. Be careful not to lose the truth in speculation. Luke's story teaches a major truth.

Jesus had moved from the synagogue to the sea shore to teach. Luke said he was on the shore of Lake Gennesaret, usually called Sea of Galilee. Galilee means circle. It is an area in northern Israel; much of it bordering the Sea of Galilee. The Sea of Galilee is about 13 miles from south to north and about 8 miles west to east. It is 700 feet below sea level. The Jordan River flows in on the north and out at the south. It was important because of the large fishing industry, but also a lot of Jesus' Galilean ministry occurs on and around it.

Jesus was on the shore, a crowd so pressed in to hear him that he borrowed Simon's boat, pushed out a bit from shore, and used the boat for his seat forteaching. Wonder what he told the crowd. Think it may have been about the love of God and the Kingdom of God?

After teaching, Jesus said to Simon, "Put out into the deep water and letdown the nets for a catch." Said Simon, the professional fisherman, to Jesus, the itinerant preacher/teacher, carpenter, "Master, we've worked hard (fished) all night long and haven't caught anything." Stop here and consider the situation. It is said that night time was the time to fish, at least that is what Simon and his crew did, now it is broad daylight; shallow water the more likely place? Jesus said go to deep water. These fishermen have been up all night and need rest to go out again when night came. Think the fishermen had some concern about this?

In future lessons you will learn that Simon Peter's mouth often got him in trouble, but not this time. Simon's answer to Jesus may be one of the best things he said. "Because you say so I will let down the nets." If you say so! Keep that in your mind. Memorize it. Say it. Say it to Jesus. If you say so I will do whatever you ask me. I trust what you say. That is the lesson. Thanks to Dr. Luke for telling this story. By the way, Luke was a physician. Colossians 4:14.

Read the rest of the story. Their nets got so full they were about to tear. They called for another boat and both boats were so full they were about to sink.

It is interesting what will cause a person to see him/herself as in need of change. Peter fell to his knees and confessed that he was a sinner. The others were amazed at the catch of fish. This was a good day for the fishing company, but Jesus was looking beyond fish. Jesus told them they would be catching people; a way of saying that they would be living and telling the good news so that others would also follow Jesus. Do you think that is what Jesus meant by saying that they would catching men?

The four left the boats, hired hands and father to follow Jesus. "If You Say So."

Application to Life

When you are faced with decisions that require choosing between right and wrong or between what "everyone does" and right, be ready with your answer, "IF YOU SAY SO, LORD."

Jesus is saying to you, "Come, follow me," That is about as good a description as you will find of being a disciple. So, what do you say? Will you follow Jesus? If you are already a follower, you know that this is a daily commitment. Every day you show by your words, deeds and thoughts that you have decided to follow him.

There is a gospel chorus with words like: I Have Decided to Follow Jesus. I have decided to follow Jesus. No turning back. No turning back. Though none go with me, I still will follow. No turning back. No turning back.

Discuss how you follow Jesus today: by the way you speak, do your job; treat your friends, family, coworkers, strangers. Make your list.

Jesus Healed a Demoniac in the Synagogue
Mark 1:21-28; Luke 4:31-37

This is the second healing story in Jesus' Galilean ministry. The first was the healing of a nobleman's son who was deathly ill (John 4:46-54). This one is the healing of a man who "was possessed by an impure spirit" (Mark 1:23). Other translations say unclean spirit. The people of that day believed that demons could inhabit persons, animals and objects. Was this impure spirit a demon? Are Mark and Luke contrasting the impure spirit with Holy God or Holy Spirit? Many thinks that we would call the demoniac mentally ill today. Would you agree? Or what do you think? Mark and Luke write almost word for word the same in this story.

The purpose of this study is not to get you to believe or not believe in impure spirits or demons. It is not to convince you that Jesus believed or did not believe in impure spirits or demons. Rather, the purpose of this lesson is to emphasize the power or authority of Jesus to release, set free, deliver a person from whatever keeps the person from wholeness. Recall Jesus read from Isaiah 58 and 61 (Luke 4:16-31). The passages tell about setting captives free.

The people recognized that Jesus spoke with authority, but the impure spirit knew Jesus to be "the Holy One of God" (Mark1:24). Jesus healed the demoniac.

A key lesson in this story is the authority or power of Jesus. He did not speak as the teachers of the law, who apparently made a habit of quoting "authoritative sources" to prove their point. Jesus spoke as one who received his words from God. In Matthew chapter 5 there are several times when Jesus said "you have heard that it was said....do not kill, steal, commit adultery.... but I say unto you. But I say to you, do not hate, do not covet, do not lust."

Read the story in Mark 2:1-12 where Jesus claims to have the **authority** to forgive sins. And in Jesus' last word recorded by Matthew (28:18) he said, "All **authority** in heaven and on earth has been given to me."

The authority is a sure sign that Jesus is the Messiah. Mark makes a point all through his Gospel that disciples, family, religious leaders have difficulty seeing him as the Christ. Even though Peter said he was the Christ, it was evident he did not understand Jesus' mission. Demons and a soldier at the crucifixion of Jesus seemed to know.

The synagogue service was disrupted when a man with an impure spirit cried out "What do you want with us, Jesus of Nazareth? Have you come to destroy us? I know who you are—the Holy One of God" (Mark 1:24). He must have known that Jesus had the authority to drive the unclean spirit from the man. That is exactly what Jesus did.

"Be quiet!" said Jesus sternly. "Come out of him!" The impure spirit shook the man violently and came out of him with a shriek; verses 25-26. Do you think Jesus, setting this man free, illustrates what Paul the Apostle meant when he wrote Romans 8:38-39?

"For I am convinced that neither death nor life, neither angels nor demons, neither present nor future, nor any powers, neither height nor depth, nor anything else in all creation, will be able to separate us from the love of God that is in Christ Jesus our Lord." These are powerful and authoritative words.

The folk left the synagogue in great awe that day. Regardless of how much they understood about the miracle they had witnessed, they told everyone they saw about it. As will be seen in future lessons, the crowds quickly increased. People wanted to see Jesus. Many, probably most, out of curiosity began gathering to places where Jesus was. They wanted to see signs and wonders done by this man named Jesus.

Application to Life

At first thought you may be asking, "What has this lesson to do with me?" But the truth is, it really has a wonderful message for everyone, where ever you live, whoever you are, there is a powerful truth for you.

Begin with a question like this. What is the controlling authority in my life? Or to make it blunter ask, to what am I addicted? "Wait a minute," you may be thinking, "I am certainly no addict." Hear me out. A demoniac is one whose life is controlled by a demon or impure spirit. An addict is one whose life is in the control of something or maybe it could be someone. Now, rethink your questions.

You may usually think of addict referring to a "drug addict." But what about power addicts, money addicts, sex addicts, fame, popularity, violence, ego addicts. You can add to the list or make your own. Do you see? Whatever you give your first loyalty to becomes the controlling influence in your life.

What about mental illness? Big strides have been made in this area in the last hundred years, but it is still a growing problem. What is the church responsibility in this area of ministry?

Jesus frees, sets free, converts, choose your word. He loves you. He shows his love through others. Support groups have shown ways of healing. A Christian friend or partner may be helpful. For help, here is a contact you can make for help. Twelve Step programs have helped thousands. They often meet in churches.

Jesus Healed Simon Peter's Mother-in-Law:
Matthew 8:14-17; Mark 1:29-39; Luke 4:38-44

This study is the third healing story in Jesus' Galilean ministry. Note the variations in the three stories. In the first (John 4:46-54), a deathly ill **child** is healed at the request of his father. Jesus proclaims him well from a distance. In the second story (Luke 4:31-37), a **man** is released from an impure spirit, even though the spirit and the man (?) protest. This takes place in a synagogue. The third story, the one for this study, is a **woman**, the mother-in-law of Simon Peter. Simoni's one of Jesus' disciples. The healing takes place in Simon's home. This variation will continue in several future studies. Watch for them, asking who, where, when, maybe how and why? You may not find answers to all five questions, but these questions can be a good tool in your Bible study. A good Bible Dictionary is one of your best tools for Bible study. So is a study Bible such as The New Interpreters Study Bible.

In this study, observe how each of the three writers gave some different information from the other two. Consider the story in three sections: Jesus had a long day; Jesus healed Simon's mother-in-law; her response to being healed.

When you read the three stories told by Mark (probably first) followed by Matthew and Luke you will see that a lot happened in one day. The speaking and healing in the synagogue were followed by going to Simon's home and healing his mother-in-law. As evening approached, a large crowd gathered bringing a host of sick people seeking to be healed. Before day the following morning Jesus leaves the house to find a quiet place for meditation and prayer. One reason for saying the day was long and tiring is from the sheer number of things he did. But more than that, there is something Jesus said in Luke 8:46: "Someone touched me, I know that power has gone out from me." Jesus was involved with those to whom he ministered. He had deep feelings for them. When he saw the people hurting, he hurt. Matthew adds a very interesting comment about Jesus' involvement in the healings. He quoted Isaiah 53:4. Read Matthew

8:17: "He took up our infirmities and bore our grief." Matthew said Jesus was fulfilling Isaiah's prophesy. What about that?

Continue noting how each writer gives a bit of information the other two do not. Mark said they went to the home of Simon and Andrew. Perhaps trivia, but did both brothers live with their mother or their mother with them? Was Andrew married? Was Peter's father alive?

They told Jesus about the illness one says, and another said Jesus saw her. And. Luke (recall in Colossian 4:14) said her fever was a **high** fever. Jesus touched her hand (Matthew) and the fever left her. He took her hand and helped her up (Mark). So, he bent over her, rebuked the fever and it left her (Luke).

In this healing we are dealing with family. Not strangers, not a crowd, just family was present. A real danger in "ministry" is to neglect the most important people in your life. Jesus did not do that. One to one ministry is the way. That is another one to factor into your studies. Watch how often Jesus is teaching or healing an individual person. His interest was in the total person and his relationship to them.

None of the writers told her age, but she could have been up in years. And having Peter as a son-in-law may have "put a lot of miles" or wrinkles on her. Be that as it may, there was and is a wonderful lesson in what she did. Interesting all three writers say the same thing about when she got up: "She began to wait on them." Therein lies the lesson to take home. The word translated "wait on" or as some translations read, "serve" is the word from which deacon comes. She was serving and that is the heart of being a disciple. Jesus served and told his followers that they were to serve others.

Application to Life

Think about, discuss and determine ways to act on the following statements or make your own list based on what you learned from the study:

Home may be your most needed place of service. What do you need to do? Be specific. For whom? When? Why? How?

Jesus was gracious in his service, but also gracious in being "waited on." Are you?

Gratitude can be expressed in service. The mother-in-law did. How can you?

Jesus needed quiet time and rest. So, do you. What are you going to do about it?

Interruptions (the crowd in the story) can become opportunities for service.

Jesus wants you to follow him. What will you do about that?

Jesus Healed a Leper
Matthew 8:1-4; Mark 1:40-45; Luke 5:12-16

Jesus continued to show his power to release persons from disease. The story for this study is very well-known story, it tells that Jesus healed a leper. The word translated leprosy used in Leviticus 13 in Hebrew and in Greek in this passage might better be translated skin disease. Leprosy today is Hansen's Disease.

Are the symptoms in Leviticus 13 those of Hansen's Disease? The disease in Leviticus would grow on cloth and stone. Like mold? Those with the disease(s) in Leviticus 13 are expected to recover. This in no way is intended to minimize the physical pain, psychological trauma, distress of appearance, social embarrassment, or religious ostracization. These were all part of the man's condition who came to Jesus in this study. In this story Jesus healed the man with "leprosy." He sent the man to the priest to be pronounced cured or clean.

If you have not read Leviticus 13, pause here to read it. It is a rather long and detailed description of skin diseases; diagnosis and not treatment, but various degrees of isolation and signs of cure. All the traumas mentioned above would apply here. The victim was cut off from worship with the congregation. He/she lived or existed outside the camp, could not come near another person and must cover his upper lip and call out "Unclean" to anyone who may be in his vision. He was ceremonially unclean to come to the place of worship. Anyone who **touched** the leper would also become unclean.

The physician, Luke said the man was covered with the disease. Three authors (Matthew, Mark and Luke) told us this story. That gives us added vision of what took place. Two say he knelt before Jesus, one says he prostrated, fell on his face before Jesus. These are signs of reverence, humility and maybe desperation. All three say the man begged for healing. "If you will?"

"If you will, you can make me clean," he said. Do we hear faith being expressed? Do you hear confidence in his request? How do you think his voice, his begging sounded? Where did his faith and confidence come from? Had he heard that Jesus healed others? Had he met one or more persons that Jesus had healed? Had someone suggested that he go to Jesus and maybe told him where he could find Jesus.

Jesus willed. Yes, Jesus was willing to make him clean, to cure him. To show it, Jesus reached out and **TOUCHED** him. That is a "No, No!" This man was an **UNTOUCHABLE** And he said to the man, "I am willing. Be clean." And the man was healed. The leprosy left him the writers say.

Jesus gave the healed man two commands. Do not tell anyone. That is a strange request and a difficult one to obey. Don't tell anyone that you have been healed of a dread disease? Why would Jesus ask this of him? Could it be that Jesus did not want to arouse the anger of the religious or civic leaders? Could it be that he knew that the people were looking for a Messiah of war and violence and he was a Christ of peace and nonviolence?

The second command; go show the priest, let the priest declare him healed, as was his job according to Leviticus. But why did Jesus do this. Maybe because Jesus was a Jew and had very high respect for Jewish law. The law was given for the welfare and guidance of the people. Whatever you decide, keep in mind throughout the study that Jesus was human as well as Divine and he was a Jew.

Application to Life

What in the world could this lesson about a skin disease being healed have for life application today? I am glad you asked. Hold on, this could be a rough ride!

Who are your untouchables? Does this sound a little like AIDS victims? You make the list.

Who are those people you want to avoid? Handicapped, special needs, those different in what way from you, who are they?

What do you know about the power of touch; appropriate, compassionate touch? When have you touched someone in that way; to say I care, I'm here, you can depend on me? Who has given you such a touch recently? Where do you not feel welcome? Why? Who is not welcome in your group? What about your church?

Think about a time when you were "left out" or not chosen. What about this week, seek out a person in need and do something that will help them: a hand on the shoulder, a smile, a word of encouragement, a note, a text, a call, etc.

Jesus Healed a Paralytic
Matthew 9:1-8; Mark 2:1-12; Luke 5:17-26

The crowds increased to hear Jesus and be healed, At the same time opposition increased. There were those who criticized him. Mark said that Jesus had come home to Capernaum. You may recall that Jesus was driven from the synagogue in his home town of Nazareth. He then moved to Capernaum on the north shore of the Sea of Galilee. In whose house he was teaching is not noted. But there was a crowd so large that it blocked the door. Luke said there were Pharisees and teachers of the law present; some from as far away as Jerusalem. He also said that the power of the Lord was present for him to heal the sick. The focus of this study is on some men who brought a paralytic to Jesus. Jesus forgave and healed the paralytic. Jesus defended his power to forgive sin and to heal. This story is filled with excitement, determination, faith and humor.

Somewhere in town one or more men knew that Jesus had returned to Capernaum. They knew he had power to heal. They had a friend who was paralyzed. They believed Jesus could heal him. They (one or more of them) had a brilliant idea. They could take him to Jesus. They placed their friend on a pallet and carried him to Jesus.

They got there late. The house was so crowded they could not even get close to the door. Determined, they climbed the outside stairs of the flat roofed house. Now it begins to get funny. They tear a hole in the roof. Was the roof clay tiles or thatch or brush and mud? It does not say; but can you imagine the confusion. Dirt, dust, debris began falling on the heads of those inside. In no time there was a three by six-foot hole above them. How big would you guess the hole was? Peering down thru the hole are four, six, you guess, faces. Then suddenly, a pallet was being lowered through the hole. They might have ropes tied to the corners, but they were not expecting this problem. Don't you expect that one or more of them shouted, "Some of ya'll help us. Catch him. We can only reach so far." Can you imagine Jesus not looking up with a huge grin or maybe a big belly laugh? The story said when Jesus saw the faith of those who brought him, he said to the paralyzed man, "Son, your sins are forgiven" (Luke 2:5). That means trouble. Remember who was present? Pharisees and law teachers; minds were spinning. Who does this man think he is, only God can forgive sins. They have heard what they came to hear. They had Jesus trapped. Jesus saw their body language and facial expressions. Before they could complain, he asked them a question. "Which is easier to say to the paralytic, 'Your sins are forgiven,' or to say, 'Get up, take up your mat and walk' But that you may know that the Son of Man has authority on earth to forgive sins…He said to the paralytic, 'Get up, take your mat and go home.'" And the man picked up his mat before the whole crowd and walked out.

Several words and ideas need to be discussed about the controversy. One is the question: Who is Jesus? Jesus calls himself Son of Man. This term is used in the Book of Daniel 7:13-14. It has the promise of the Son of Man who will have an eternal kingdom consisting of all nations and peoples. Did the Pharisees hear Jesus claiming then to be the Christ? A second problem was the belief about sin and sickness. There was a strong belief then and now that if a person was ill, it was caused by the person's sin. This can be and is often true. But diseases have multiple causes. The sin of one person can affect another, it is important not to hurt people using words as weapons. The point here is that the person is more important than what caused the illness. Jesus' concern was to heal. If sin is the cause, he forgives. Forgiveness can be a vital factor in personal healing. You may need to forgive, or you may need forgiving.

So, the story ended with jeers from some but cheers from the crowd. They had never seen such a sight. Don't forget, people are a priority in the ministry of Jesus.

Application to Life

How do the knowledge, skills, discoveries, in modern medicine relate to God's healing? Is all truth from God? A person, then and now, is a whole being: mentally, physically, socially, and psychologically. All these are bound up in the person and every area affects other areas. Much illness is psychosomatic. Can you name diseases that are related to stress, bad habits, poor nutrition, or bad environment? Do you think Christians should be interested in these matters? List ways you and your church can work in the healing and forgiving ministry.

Jesus Called Levi
Matthew 9:9-17; Mark 2:13-22; Luke 5:27-39

Matthew was a tax collector in the city of Capernaum, the city where Jesus lived. It was on the northern shore of the lake called the Sea of Galilee.

As a tax collector for the Roman government, Matthew collected various import and export tariffs from local citizens and foreigners. Tax collectors had a bad reputation for over charging and were sometimes called traitors by the Jewish people. Living in the city of Capernaum, Matthew must have heard Jesus teach and knew about some of the miracles that Jesus performed in the Capernaum. Jesus had healed a Roman soldier's servant, he had healed Simon Peter's mother in law and a paralytic was healed when four friends brought him to Jesus. When they got to where Jesus was teaching, the crowd was so big that they could not get to the door. So, they took the man to the flat roof up outside stairs; pulled back some of the thatched roof and lowered the man with ropes down into Jesus presence. Jesus stopped his teaching and healed the man. Read these stories and that of Jesus calling Matthew to be his disciple in the Gospel of Matthew chapters 8 and 9.

According to the stories, Jesus went to Matthew's tax booth. We would probably think of it as Matthew's office. There Jesus gives him the invitation he had given others, "Come, follow me." A classic painting by Caravaggio called "The Calling of Saint Matthew."

Find the painting up on your computer and study it. He depicts Jesus and Simon Peter pointing at Matthew as the tax collector and his Associates sit around a table apparently counting their money. They are dressed in fine clothes of the day as Jesus and Peter stand there with bare feet and clothes that contrast with the finery of the tax collectors. Matthew is seen pointing a finger at himself with a silent expression that says, "Who, me?" as he clutches his money in the other hand. The painting hangs in the Church of Saint Louis of France in the city of Rome.

This was a major decision time for Matthew and probably caused a real tension in his life. This was a life changing decision, weather to follow Jesus into an unknown future or remain in the financial security of his tax collecting. Surely, he had already given serious thought to this option. Perhaps he knew some of those who had already been called by Jesus to follow him, that is to become his follower and learn from him. However, we might speculate about this, the scripture says that Matthew got up, left his business and followed Jesus.

You may also find it interesting that Matthew immediately planned a banquet for Jesus and invited his fellow tax collector friends and others to attend. No doubt he did this for several reasons. He wanted them to meet Jesus for themselves. He wanted his friends to know he had decided to follow Jesus. And he saw this as an opportunity for Jesus to speak to some people that might not go to where Jesus was preaching. The fact is we know that the event took place and Jesus was there.

But others came to cause trouble. Some religious persons came with questions. Why would Jesus, if he was the Messiah, go to the home of a sinner and even eat in his home with other persons of questionable character?

The questions simply gave Jesus the opportunity to express the love of God by telling them that God had sent him to save those who recognized they were sinners and in need of God. He did not mean that God did not love those who were critical of him, but he was trying to show them that all are sinners and need to recognize and receive the love of God. Their attitude of superiority showed that they had a faulty idea about God. God loves, and Jesus died for the whole creation.

Note one other thing about Matthew and his call. Matthew would later write the first book in the New Testament of the Bible, The Gospel According to Matthew. Do you suppose Jesus saw this talent of Matthew to keep records and write?

Matthew in deciding to follow Jesus, used his talents to serve others.

Application to Life

So, what does the call of Jesus to Matthew, "Come, follow me," have to do with you? EVERYTHING!!!The same Jesus who invited Matthew to be his disciple, also calls You to be his disciple. What does this mean in everyday language? Here are several suggestions on getting started on a lifelong adventure with Jesus.

You will want to learn all you can about Jesus. Disciple means learner. Hopefully this study will help.

List your gifts or talents. How are you using them to serve others?

Jesus Healed a Lame Man
John 5:1-47

Three observations need to be made at the beginning of this study.

Jesus was in Jerusalem for a Jewish religious festival and worship. The text does not say which festival, but this means many people were there.

Why is this study included in a study of Jesus' Galilean ministry? In trying to "harmonize" the stories of the four gospels, the story fits here. John chapter five is a long story which only John recorded. Because of limited space for this study, not all the verses will be discussed. John used the word Jews in the same way the other gospel writers used the words; Pharisees, teachers of the law, etc.; that is Jewish religious leaders. That does not mean all the religious leaders agreed.

Warning: Do not think of all Jews as opposed to Jesus. Jesus also was a Jew.

The study falls into three parts: Jesus healed a lame man; Jesus was accused by religious authorities; and Jesus defended his person and work.

The temple in Jerusalem included a huge court yard area. Near the "Sheep Gate" was a pool. It was surrounded by a covered area. In this area a crowd of sick, lame and other handicapped people gathered to wait for the water in the pool to "stir." The first into the pool, when it was stirred by an angel, was healed. That is the way some told the story. Was that superstition? Jesus saw a man and learned that he had been lame for thirty-eight years. Jesus asked the man an unusual question, "Do you want to get well?" Don't you find that strange? Would you ask a patient that question? What do you think Jesus knew about the man? Could it be that he did not want to get well? Why? The man did not answer the question but made excuse that he had no one to help him into the water. How did he get to the pool? Would someone carry him there day after day and not have time to wait?

Jesus told the man to "Get up, take up your mat and walk." The man did. But religious leaders saw the man and confronted him about breaking the law by carrying his mat on the Sabbath. He was doing what "some man" told him to do.

Jesus found the man and told him to sin no more. The man learned Jesus name and went to tell the religious authorities. What do you think about that?

The religious leaders began to persecute Jesus. Why would he break Sabbath law? One of the Ten Commandments reads: "Remember the Sabbath day by keeping it holy" Exodus 20:8. Religious leaders had added dozens of things that could not be done on Sabbath. How far a person could walk, how much weight one could carry' etc. No one had more respect for the law and obeyed it better than Jesus. But man-made additions, traditions, and such could not bind him. Jesus saw human beings as a priority of his ministry.

In this section Jesus gave four witnesses to his authority and person. The first was John the Baptist. More than once Jesus referred John's witness to him (John 1:19-35). Second, Jesus said his own works testified to who he was. Third, Jesus said God, his Father, gave his approval. Fourth, Jesus told them to read the scripture, which would be the Old Testament. Moses, whom they revered for giving the law, and the prophets spoke of him.

Application to Life

Fear of change and losing position caused the religious leaders to attack Jesus. How do fear and jealousy affect your relationship to others? Think about and discuss the bravery of Jesus in this story. Do you speak and do what is right even if you know there is opposition?

Jesus Healed a Man with a Shriveled Hand
Matthew 12:1-14; Mark 3:1-6; Luke 6:6-11

As you begin this study, review the previous studies in this series to see the variety of people and diseases healed. A boy near death, the name of the disease was not recorded, see John 4:46. A man with an impure spirit was healed, see Mark 1:21. A mother-in-law with a high fever, see Luke 4:38. A man with a skin disease (leper) was not allowed to touch or be touched, see Luke 5:12. A paralyzed man was carried by his friends to Jesus, see Luke 5:17. A lame man was healed, see John 5. In this lesson Jesus heals a man with a shriveled hand. Some translations read withered hand. Did you notice the variety? Does this point to Jesus' concern for the wellbeing of all kinds of people? Does it mean Jesus is concerned about mental, physical, and spiritual health? Does salvation have to do with the total person in his/her total relationships? Jesus came to forgive sin and to show the way to wholeness of life.

Be aware of how wonderfully the gospel writers (Matthew, Mark, Luke and John) compliment, supplement and bring to the stories an array of viewpoints.

In this story Jesus challenges the religious traditions and healed the man with the shriveled hand in the synagogue on the Sabbath.

Jesus was teaching in a synagogue on the Sabbath. A man with a shriveled hand was there. Pharisees and scribes (teachers of the law) were there. Reminder: these Jewish religious leaders were very sincere followers of the law of Moses and the 613 additions; interpretations made into rules. They had a problem with Jesus because they did not believe he had proper respect for those 613 rules. Jesus was a Jew and believed very strongly in the law but did not feel bound by traditions. As we will study in later lessons Jesus summed up the whole law in two commands. Love God with all your being and love your neighbor as yourself. See Mark 12:28-31.

Matthew said the Pharisees asked Jesus, "Is it lawful to heal on the Sabbath?" Mark and Luke record that Jesus asked them that question. Read Luke 12:8-9: "But Jesus knew what they were thinking and said to the man with the shriveled hand, 'Get up and stand in front of everyone.' So, he got up and stood there. "Do you think Jesus was challenging them? Did Jesus show courage to have the man stand in front of the congregation, knowing that he was going to heal him and inflame the anger of his adversaries?

It may have been at this time in the event Jesus said, "If any of you has a sheep and it falls into a pit on the Sabbath, will he not take hold of it and lift it out? How much more value is a man than a sheep? Therefore, it is lawful to do good on the Sabbath." Matthew 12:11-12. Jesus told the man to stretch forth his hand. He did, and it was made whole like the other hand. Luke, a physician, observes that it was his right hand that was shriveled and was healed. That is an interesting addition. Does that say his hand for making a living had been restored? A traditional story said that the man was a stone cutter. Be that as it may, he needed his right hand for a lot of reasons. This should have been a joyful and grateful occasion for all. Surely it was for the healed man, his family and friends. But Jesus' adversaries were furious. They left the synagogue and began discussing how they might destroy Jesus. Amazing what fear, jealousy, bigotry can do to good people.

Application to Life

Make a list of how hands can be used in service to others and thus to God.

Make another list of attitudes and "impure spirits" that "shrivel" (metaphor) hands and cause them not to be of service.

God asked Moses on one occasion, "What is that in your hand?" (Exodus 4:2).

Read the story in Exodus chapters 3 and 4. What excuses did Moses use? What are your excuses? What traditions can get in the way of service?

Jesus Selected 12 Apostles
Matthew 12:15-21; Mark 3:7-19; Luke 6:12-16

This study is far more than a list of 12 men selected from a crowd of Jesus 'followers. The what, why, when, etc. approach may be a good way to organize this study. Two words need defining. Disciple means learner or follower. Here, to learn and be like Jesus. Apostle means one sent, as on a mission. So, these selected 12 disciples will be called apostles, Mark 3:14 says, "He (Jesus) appointed twelve – designating them apostles – that they might be with him and that he might send them out to preach "Be with him as disciples, send them out as apostles. Jesus had several disciples, men and women, Luke 8:1-3. The 12may have reflected the twelve tribes of Israel. Also, in current small group adult education, twelve is a good group number. Interesting? Now to the **what.**

Read again Luke 4:16-31. Jesus saw the Messiah (Christ) mission to release the captives (literal and/or metaphorical), preach good news to the poor, give sight to the blind, proclaim the year of the Lord's favor. Or read John 10:10, "I am come that they might have life, and have it to the full." However, you interpret it, Jesus gave his life even to death to save the world from whatever was/is keeping it from living life here and hereafter as God intended. His mission was to proclaim "The Kingdom (reign) of God is here, now and future. Repent, turn around and follow Jesus' way of love.

Why Did Jesus Select 12 Apostles?

Knowing this, Jesus knew his death was near and his mission must be continued. His approach was to choose twelve men to train as apostles to carry on the mission.

When Did Jesus Select 12 Apostles?

This question is not to date but like why**,** there was some urgency. They had been in training. It was time to practice what they had learned from Jesus.

Where Did Jesus send the 12 Apostles?

The first mission was local. But Jesus words after his resurrection to them were, Matthew 28:19: "Therefore, go and make disciples of all nations...."

How Were the Disciple to Do the Mission?

Preaching the Good News, the gospel, God loves you, you are forgiven, turn and follow Jesus. Preach by word and life. John 13:35, "By this will all men know you are my disciples, if you love one another." As you will note, learning who these characters were, the twelve was an experiment in community. As the world, so the church, the apostles were a mixed bunch who had to learn to love one another.

Who Were the 12 Apostles?

Here is a word about each and some references to read more. For some, all we know is their name on the list. A few will show up often in the Gospels and other New Testament books. So, watch for them. twelve ordinary men selected by Jesus.

Simon Peter and Andrew were brothers and fishermen, John 1:40; Mark 10:28; Mark 9:2-8; 11:21.

James and John were also brothers and fishermen. Mark 9:2; 3:17; 5:37 9:2-8; Mark 14:32-33.

Philip John 1:43-51; 6:5-7; 12:21-22.

Matthew was a tax collector. He threw a party for Jesus and wrote a Gospel.

Thomas was brave and a seeker of truth. Mark 3:18; John 11:16; 20:25-28.

Simon the Zealot was of a group committed to kill Romans, changed by Jesus.

James the Less may have been short of statue or younger than the other James.

Bartholomew may be another name for Nathanael **Thaddaeus** is the other Judas and/or James in some lists? **Judas Iscariot** John 12:5-6; 13:18-30.

Application to Life

Take time to read about each disciple. Use a Bible Dictionary if available. In which of the disciples do you see characteristics of yourself? Discuss. What training do you need to be a better disciple? Discuss the importance of including different kinds of people in your life and church.

Jesus Gave the Sermon on the Mount
Matthew 5:1-48; 6:1-34; 7:1-29; Luke 6:17-49

These are three of the most important chapters in the Bible. The chapters together are called the Sermon on the Mount. The sermon could be called the constitution of the Kingdom of God. It tells how to live on earth, present time, as well as when it was spoken, in relationship with oneself, God and others. Though you will recognize over laps and back and forth, the lesson will attempt to deal with how to relate to yourself, chapter 5; how to relate to God, chapter 6; and how to relate to others, chapter 7. The lesson will suggest that verse 48 is the key verse for chapter five; Verse 33 for chapter 6; and verse 12 for chapter 7.

You may recall in an earlier study that life is relationships. You can't avoid them. This lesson hopefully will challenge you to see that life is a never-ending task of growing or declining in relationships.

He began with what are called the BEATITUDES, 5:3-11. The word is translated blessed or happy. Blessed is the person who is **poor in spirit**. Could this be persons who know that they are dependent upon God and fellow human beings? Not arrogant proud or boastful. Those who **mourn;** could this be people who really care about pain and grief of others? Not persons who close their eyes to the needs of others. Blessed are the **meek;** not weak. These are ones who have control of their emotions and abilities. The word picture is a horse which has come under the control of a master. Those who hunger for **justice** or righteousness; that is, they are active in doing and desiring right for others. Could **pure in heart** have to do with pure motivation? **Peacemakers**, active not passive, are those who act for peace for all, beginning at home. The **persecuted for doing right** are those who return good for evil.

Then two metaphors are given, salt and light. These suggest that Jesus' followers are to be healers, preservers, direction setters, examples of those described above. Then Jesus described his love for the Jewish law, but emphasized that right doing begins in the heart, will, and motivation. Read the examples: the law says do not kill, commit adultery, but Jesus said do not hate and lust. Some of the things like turn the other cheek, are not weakness, but a way of standing up to hostility in a way that says I too am a human being. Love your enemies? Did he mean, "Care for all people?"

Three major religious practices of the Jewish religion were giving alms and other acts of piety, prayer, and fasting. All three could be used as show and performance for the praise and admiration of man; wrong motive. Jesus taught that relationship with God is personal, private. Sure, there should be prayer with others and deeds of righteousness are going to be seen. The point is, why are you doing it? Note that Matthew included the model prayer in this section. Note the plural pronouns all through the prayer, Our Father, our daily bread, our trespasses.

Trust is an added subject. Do not let the cares of life eat you up. Remember you belong to God. He loves you. "Consider the birds" did not mean do not work. Who works harder than birds? Remember your relationship of trust in God to guide. The key to help with peacefulness and right motive is verse 33, "But seek first his kingdom and his righteousness, and all these things will be given to you as well."

Do not judge. Do not be a fault finder. Consider your own wrongs, they may be far worse that the one you find fault with. But he also says beware of those who deal in lies. They key verse is 12, "So in everything, do unto others what you would have them do to you, for this is the Law and the Prophets." This has been called, "The Golden Rule." The Jewish Rabbi would teach, "Do not do to others what you do not want them to do to you." Jesus made it positive and active. Be reminded of the words of Jesus about the Law: "Love the Lord your God with all your heart and with all your soul and with all your mind. This is the first and greatest commandment. And the second is like it: Love your neighbor as yourself. All the Law and Prophets hang on these two commandments," Matthew 22:37-40. The first is a quote from Deuteronomy 6:5 and the second from Leviticus 19:18. Right out of Jewish Law.

Application to Life

Compare and discuss the similarities and differences of Luke's shorter version of the sermon recorded by Matthew. Was Luke just using parts of Matthew's account? Luke recorded the model prayer in chapter 11. Compare the two prayers.

Discuss each of the beatitudes. Do you agree or disagree with the lesson writer?

Discuss proper motives for religious acts such as prayer, giving, helping.

Discuss what your group should do in areas such as peacemaking and justice.

Discuss how following Jesus is a lifelong path, but a path of joy and peace.

Jesus Healed a Centurion's Servant
Matthew 8:5-13; Luke 7:1-10

This is a good study to follow the Sermon on the Mount Matthew chapters five, six and seven and Luke chapter 6. Matthew and Luke placed the story right after the sermon. They both had Jesus back in Capernaum. This story showed that Jesus practiced what he preached. Watch for things like loving your enemy, caring for the poor and single heartedness. Jesus healing a centurion's servant is like the first Galilean ministry story of Jesus healing the nobleman's son (John 4:46-54).

The persons in this story are Jesus, a Roman centurion, Jewish elders and a slave of the centurion. There are slight differences in the stories. Matthew said the Centurion came to Jesus. Luke said that he sent Jewish elders (religious leaders) to Jesus. **The entire story is filled with contrasts. There are contrasts in the characters, vocations, motives, authority and power.**

The Roman centurion was a Roman soldier assigned to Capernaum. He oversaw one hundred soldiers. Centurions seem to have made a good impression on New Testaments writers. When Jesus was crucified, Mark 5:39 read, "When the centurion who stood there in front of Jesus, heard the cry and saw how he died, he said, 'Surely this man was the Son of God.'" Read also Acts chapter ten and the book of Acts chapter twenty-seven. What do you know about the centurion in this lesson? He was Gentile, high ranking soldier with authority and power from the emperor, he had wealth. He built the Jews a synagogue. He was trained for violence and war. He owned slave(s), was good to Jews in Capernaum. He had faith. Do you know more?

Jesus was a Jew, as carpenter and itinerant preacher/healer, some thought him to be the Messiah. He had no wealth, had some volunteer followers, he preached and practiced equality of all people and nonviolence, he claimed the power of God.

In the interchange of Jesus and the centurion notice some great similarities. Both had faith, both cared for the slave, both respected the other as a human being. Whether the centurion came in person or sent the elders, he had a deep concern for the ill slave and that is to be commended. Slavery was a part of the culture of the world at that time. It is still practiced in many ways and places today, even though for Christians and all people it should be a major evil.

The centurion knew it would be against tradition for Jesus to enter a Gentile home. Jesus was on his way and no doubt would have entered the centurion's home. The centurion recognized power and authority in Jesus, for he, himself, had power and authority of another kind. Jesus spoke the word and the servant was healed, just as the centurion believed he would be healed.

Jesus paid a high compliment to the centurion in Luke 7:9, "I tell you, I have not found such great faith even in Israel." After a similar comment by Matthew he used the metaphor of a feast (at the end time?) of the kingdom of heaven. Many unexpected guests are there from the east and west; and some, expected, fail to show. Does this speak of abused privilege and the inclusiveness of God's grace? Faith is more important than race, nationality, creeds, sexuality. God loves all mankind.

A word about motive could be said here about the Jewish elders. Without being judgmental toward them, because neither gospel said what motivated them; could they have been motivated by the building given them by the centurion rather than the servant and his condition? Were they friends of the centurion for the same reason? Just a thought to prompt self-examination as to motive for things done by us.

The passage following in Luke said that John the Baptist's disciples told John about this and how excited the people were. John sent two of his disciples to ask Jesus, "Are you the one who was to come, or should we expect someone else?" verse 20. Jesus said, Go back and report to John what you have seen and heard: 'the blind receive their sight, the lame walk, those who have leprosy are cured, the deaf hear, the dead are raised, and the good news is preached to the poor' verses 22,23. The kingdom comes not through violence but love in action.

Application to Life

How would you compare the power of Jesus to that of the soldier? What about the source of the power of each?

How do you see acting in love to respond to violence?

Do you think God is partial to one nation, class of people, race, sex?

Does God really love all people? Does he expect you to attempt that?

How would you improve on this definition of love: "Love is the active concern for the good of self and others?"

Jesus Raised a Widow's Son from the Dead
Luke 7:11-17

Luke was a gentile physician and believed to be the writer of the gospel bearing his name. He tells several wonderful stories not found in the other three gospels in the New Testament. This is one of those stories. It is filled with powerful symbols and practical life service. It takes place just outside the gates of Nain (word means pleasant). This is in the same area as Shine in the Old Testament. There Elisha raised a Shunammite mother's son back to life, 2 Kings 4:18-37.

Watch for: two processions; Jesus and followers meet a funeral procession. Jesus raised a dead man to life; he gave the son back to his mother; and Jesus made known that he was the Messiah (Christ).

Jesus was proceeding toward Nain with a large crowd consisting of the Twelve disciples and other followers. No doubt there were seekers for truth and curiosity seekers in the crowd. It became more and more prominent that in the crowds were those seeking reason to accuse and do Jesus harm.

Jesus' procession could be called a parade of life, marching toward death. His opposition was increasing at such a rate that he could be considered already on his march to Jerusalem and crucifixion. Luke noted this in chapter nine.

The other procession leaving Nain is a funeral procession; a parade of death. It was marching, unknowingly to life, not a grave. This procession was led by mourners wailing and crying. Following was the bier, upon which the dead man lay. Then came the dead man's mother, a widow, family and friends. The widow had made this march before with her dead husband.

The two processions met on the road. Jesus saw, he felt the pain, he touched, he spoke and gave life. Good Bible study takes notice of verbs, the action words.

Jesus saw a grieving widow whose heart was broken over her dead son. He saw a widow whose source of support and help was gone. He felt with and for her. He spoke to her. "Don't cry." Careful about using that quote to one grieving, unless you are going to raise their dead. Crying is a curative part of grief. But Jesus was going to raise her son. He touched the bier, the processions stopped. Jesus spoke to the corpse. "Young man, I say to you, get up."And the man sat up and talked.

The miracle turned practical; as practical as putting bread on her table. Jesus was not only giving her back the love of her life. He cared about her practical needs and physical wellbeing. He was giving her son back as her provider.

Just a thought. Not long from that time, Jesus would be dying on a Roman crucifix. It was then that he looked at John and gave his own mother, Mary into his care. Jesus cared for the needs of his mother. Read John 19:25-27.

In the passage following this lesson, John the Baptist sent two of his disciples to ask Jesus if he was the Messiah. Jesus told them to tell John what they had seen and heard. Remember Jesus quoting Isaiah in Luke 4:16-30? He was a nonviolent Messiah; one who would die but be raised to life; one that would give hope and promise of life to all.

Application to Life

Discuss with your group how you can be good comforters for those in grief. Do a study on how to minister to persons in grief. Grief can last a longtime. Think of those you know who have lost loved ones in the past year. What can you do for them. Do you have poor widows and widowers to whom you need to minister? Find out their needs and get your group to join you in meeting some of the needs.

Jesus Was Anointed by a Sinful Woman
Luke 7:36-50

Luke, the physician and writer of the Gospel of Luke, often added descriptive words to the diagnosis of maladies in addition to ones given by Mark and Matthew. But this is one of several stories only found in Luke. In this story Luke gave a strong diagnosis of the whole being of the personalities involved. For similar diagnoses read the story in Luke 18:9-14. Reminder: Pharisee is a word often used to describe a hypocritical person. Jesus called some of them hypocrites in Matthew 15:7. In chapter 23 of Matthew strong woes are spoken to hypocrites. Some did act from wrong motives and "holier than thou" attitudes. But as "separated ones" they were very good people, trying to keep the laws and traditions of Moses.

The story for this lesson took place in the home of a Pharisee. He had invited Jesus to his home for a meal. Eastern culture of that day would have had the host, Simon the Pharisee, give the guest, Jesus, a kiss of peace. A servant would have washed the guest's feet. And some say fragrant incense would have burned in the dining area. The unnamed woman in the story was an uninvited guest. Of these three characters: Simon judged Jesus and the woman; Jesus pronounced judgment for Simon and forgiveness for the woman; the woman showed repentance.

The opening scene had the Pharisee reclining at the dining table. Their feet would have been stretched out behind them. Supported by the left elbows, they ate with their right hands. The woman would be standing behind Jesus. Her hair had been unbraided and hung loose. She had in hand an expensive jar or vial of perfume. As she wept, she washed Jesus' feet with her tears. She dried them with her hair. And she anointed him with the perfume. Take a moment and let that picture burn itself into your mind. Would you guess the number of customs she broke? As a woman was it alright to be there? What about her known "sinful" life? What about her veil, her hair, her kissing Jesus? What do you suppose the perfume cost? And where did she get the money to buy it? What was her trade?

"When the Pharisee who had invited him saw this, he said to himself, 'If this man were a prophet, he would know who is touching him and what kind of woman; that she is a sinner'" (7:39). In one sentence he has judged Jesus and the woman. He said that Jesus could not be a prophet. Would this carry the idea, "much less the Christ?" The woman is judged by "what kind of woman" she is, that is a sinner.

Did he expect Jesus to tell her to stop; or ask the host to throw her out? Could this have been a trap to see what Jesus would do? Jesus did have women followers.

Jesus knew Simon's thoughts and told him a story about two debtors. One owed little, the other a huge debt. Both were forgiven, who will love the most? Simon's answer was as Jesus expected. Simon may have immediately seen where Jesus was leading him but answered that he supposed the one who owed most. Jesus said he gave the right answer. Then Jesus proceeded to expose Simon, who as the host, did not kiss his guest, wash his feet, or anoint him? But look who did it with extravagance. That one, the woman, had shown by her actions of gratitude that she had experienced forgiveness. Her perfume, to entice, was turned into a gift of thanks.

Did you hear her say she repented? No. But her actions speak of a changed life. Custom and tradition could not keep her from the one who forgave. Gratitude is the response to grace. Had the woman heard Jesus speak? Had she met him? The story does not say, but her actions of turn around, of a changed life say that somewhere she got the message, "God Loves You and He Has Forgiven You!!!" Tears of joy, acts of a servant, extravagant giving all say gratitude for grace received.

Application to Life

Discuss why the woman may have been a "sinner" (prostitute may be inferred). Are the reasons the same today in your culture? Are women given equal rights? Are they treated as equals in the home, workplace, church, where else?

How often do you feel, speak or act like Simon? Do you respect all persons? List ways you and your group can befriend those who are treated as "second class citizens."

Jesus Healed a Blind and Mute Man
Matthew 12:22-43; Mark 3:19-30

One rule for good Bible study is to read and interpret in context. That is, read the surrounding passages of the one you are studying. This lesson is a good example. Reading before and after, you see Jesus' enemies were increasing. Why would they not be thankful for the good work he was doing? They had seen him heal diseases. They had seen him cast out demons. Yet they refused to "see and speak" the truth about him. They would not accept him as the Christ from God. The healing in this passage is highly symbolic of their self-inflicted "blindness and muteness." In this study:

Jesus healed a blind and mute man; he reasoned with his enemy; he illustrated his reasoning; he pleaded with his enemy to see and speak the truth. Jesus was doing the work of God.

The background (context) for this passage is the story of Jesus healing the withered hand of a man. The Pharisees were so angry they conspired how they could destroy Jesus. So, he left, but continued to heal as he traveled. He told those he healed not to make him known (12:15-16). Do you think he did this so that he would have time to finish the work he planned? He knew that they did not understand his nonviolent idea of the Messiah (Christ). He was demonstrating for all to see how life was to be lived in the Kingdom of God.

He went home to Capernaum (Mark 3:19-20). A blind and mute man was brought to him. He healed the man so that he could see and speak. The crowd was amazed and recognized the Messianic characteristics of his deeds. They asked, among themselves, if this could be the promised son of David.

But the Pharisees said Jesus was doing this in the power of Beelzebul, lord of evil, or Satan. They refused to see the work of God or speak the truth about Jesus. He tried to reason with them:

1. If a kingdom is divided against its self, it cannot stand.
2. If Jesus was casting out demons in the power of Satan, by whom were they casting out demons.

3. If Satan was working against himself his kingdom was doomed.
4. But if Jesus was working in God's power, the Kingdom of God had come among them.

Jesus spoke of two Old Testament stories and characters that were witnesses against his enemies. Just like Jonah, a prophet, who spent three days in the belly of a big fish, Jesus would spend three days in the grave. They would come to see this after Jesus' resurrection.

The second story is of the Queen of Sheba who was overwhelmed by the wisdom of Solomon. Jesus was greater than both, but they rejected him.

Things had become so dangerous for Jesus and some thought he had gone "mad." His mother and brothers came to try to take him home. That is the next study. Read what Jesus said in Matthew 12:46-50; Mark 3:31-35; Luke 8:19-21.

Application to Life

Can you think of ways that you are unwilling to see new truth? How unwilling are you to change your way of thinking? Does everyone have to agree with you? All truth is from God. How do you see Jesus as the Savior of the world? Pray this old hymn:

"Open my eyes that I may see, glimpses of truth Thou hast for me. Open my mouth and let me bear, gladly your warm truth everywhere. Silently now I wait for Thee, Ready my God, thy will to see. Open my heart, illumine me, Spirit divine". Amen.

Jesus' Mother and Brothers Tried to Take Jesus Home
Matthew 12:46-50; Mark 3:31-35; Luke 8:19-21

Family is the most important relationship a person has under God; and it can be the most difficult relationship. From what we are told of Joseph, Mary, Jesus' brothers and sisters there is no reason not to believe that Jesus grew up in a good family. In fact, he remained with his family until he was about thirty years old. So, what is going on in the story for this lesson? Three of the Gospels tell the story of Jesus' mother and brothers attempting to take him home. He was teaching and healing. Why did they try to stop him? That is the first question. Second, how did Jesus describe another kind of family?

For the first question, Mark 3:21 gives us part of the answer. Some were saying, "He is out of his mind." Another translation says, "He has gone mad." These words had gotten to Jesus' family. If they had heard those words, they had also heard of plans by some of the religious leaders to have him arrested and punished,

They were accusing him of breaking religious law and traditions. He healed on the Sabbath day; he told a healed man to carry his pallet (work) on the Sabbath. Really disturbing to his enemies was Jesus' popularity with the people, who were wondering if Jesus was the Messiah (Christ). The religious leaders were jealous for their position, prestige and power. Therefore, his family came to rescue him, because they knew he could be in real trouble. They were doing what today might be called an intervention. There was a crowd gathered to hear Jesus, his family could not get to him. Word was passed through the crowd to Jesus that his mother and brothers were there and wished to speak with him. No doubt Jesus knew why they had come. Reread what Jesus said. "Who is my mother, and who are my brothers? Here are my mother and brothers (he pointed to his disciples). For whoever does the will of my Father in heaven is my brother and sister and mother" (Matthew 12:48-50). "Whoever does God's will is my brother and sister and mother" (Mark 3:35). "My mother and brothers are those who hear God's word and put it into practice" (Luke 8:21). What do you think he meant?

Jesus was not disowning his family. You can be sure of that. Even on the cross he committed his mother to the care of John (John 19:25-27). But Jesus was teaching of a higher relationship, relationship of faith in God. That relationship supersedes all others and gives true meaning to all other relationships, especially, the family. What do Jesus words about knowing and doing God's will say to us today? Are we back to Jesus' first and great commandment? "Love the Lord your God with all your heart and with all your soul and with all your mind" (Matthew 22:37).

One way of describing this relationship is by using the word love as an acrostic. Read this one and then add to it or make your own. It may help to think of God as a Father. One who desires the best relationship for you with your earthly family.

L is for listening to the word of God. You hear it through the Bible. Sometimes God speaks through friends, circumstances, reading, nature or the voice of conscience. Jesus said his Spirit would guide us into truth. His Spirit lives within you.

O is for obedience to what you understand to be God's will. For good examples of obedience read the book of James in the New Testament and Romans chapter 12.

V is for vulnerability. When you love you become transparent, you open yourself to God and others. It is risky to trust others. Jesus lived that way.

E is for encouragement and equality. Jesus loved all people and we are to learn how to encourage others and treat all people with respect. It is a daily experience.

Application to Life

Make your own or have your group do an acrostic for the word Love or Family. Most important is for you to accept God's acceptance of you as his child. Think of ways you can be of encouragement to others; be specific, names and action.

Jesus Taught by Parables
Matthew 13:1-58; Mark 4:1-34; Luke 8:1-18

You may have noticed, if you have studied the previous lessons, that there have been very few lengthy passages of Jesus' teaching. In most of the stories we have been told that he was teaching, though there were no long passages of his teaching. Jesus was a master teacher and story teller. In fact, parables are stories. The word means to throw down beside. Parables may have one central truth, but in this study, the first story is interpreted as an allegory by Jesus. That is, every part carried a meaning.

For a little Bible history on parables read the parable told by the prophet Nathan to king David, 2 Samuel 12:1-10. Note how David was "blindsided" by the parable. He didn't realize "he was the man." Another example is the Book of Jonah. What a story. In this story Jonah knew that God loved the hated Ninevites but was more concerned for his own comfort and did not want to repent of his hatred. Parables hide truth from those unwilling to see. They reveal the truth to those with "eyes to see and ears to hear." Those who seek truth. As in the stories mentioned above, so with Jesus, parables can use familiar language and common objects and situations.

All three Gospels in this lesson tell about the same stories, but Matthew tells more. Matthew will be followed to find truth in parables that say the Kingdom of God is like: extravagant sowing; good and bad seed; mustard seed and yeast; worthy treasures.

The first parable is interpreted by Jesus,13:18-23. The sower is extravagant. He must have had plenty of seed. He threw or broadcast the seed everywhere. They fell on four different soils. This is taken by many to say that there are four kinds of hearers and everyone does not respond alike, and everyone lives with different circumstances. Even the best hearers have different amounts of yield. Now read the parable and think of your own life. How is your life like all four soils? You have heard and really didn't let it sink in; sometimes you hear and get excited and soon, you have lost your excitement. You hear with good intentions of doing, but you get interested in other things. And even when you really try to obey you find the results vary. Bottom line is that God sowed, is sowing, and will sow seeds of love on all.

In the second parable God is the sower of good seed. But then comes the evil one who shows bad seed in the same field. Some scholars say that the plants even look alike. Could Jesus be saying in this parable: the world is like that? But you are not to be judges and weed pullers. You are to grow and mature as seed of love. Leave the judgment to God. The world and the people belong to him.

Do the next parables say that small things can become great and important? And, something small and hidden permeates the whole mass? The small mustard seed hidden in the earth sprouts and grows so big birds from everywhere come to it for shelter. A bit of yeast put in a bowl of flour spreads throughout the whole lump of dough unseen, but with total change in the character of the bread.

The treasure hidden in the field but found; the valuable pearl; and a drag net full offish all speak of that which is valuable. The value is so great that one sells the farm to buy it. Recall Matthew 6:33, "But seek first his kingdom and his righteousness and all things will be given to you as well." The mystery of the Kingdom of God; do you think it is Jesus, himself? His life, death, and resurrection for the whole world?

Application to Life

What hinders your growth as a person? What do the soils say about the response Jesus got to his teaching? What about response others may give you? Do you see all four soils in yourself? Write down the answer.

Have you thought about systemic or institutional or societal evil as in governments and corporations? How do the mustard seed and yeast encourage you? What is your greatest value in life? Who is the love of your life? Is God the source of all love?

Jesus Stilled the Storm at Sea
Matthew 8:18-27; Mark 4:35-41; Luke 8:22-25

Following Jesus' teaching by parables to a large crowd and interaction with some would be followers, he and the disciples got into a boat to cross the Sea of Galilee. Jesus was tired from the long day's work and went to sleep. The Sea of Galilee is about thirteen miles in length, south to north. It is about eight miles wide, west to east. It was not unusual for the normally calm lake to have sudden violent, but short-lived storms. It was such a storm that they experienced. Matthew uses the work seism's, which can be translated earth quake.

The disciples were scared witless. It must have been some storm. Recall some of these disciples were professional fishermen. They made their living fishing this very lake. They knew when to be afraid. They awakened Jesus with their shouts. They used words that sound like blame. "Teacher, don't you care if we drown?" (Mark 4:38) Jesus arose, spoke to the wind and the storm ceased. Jesus rebuked the disciples for their lack of faith. What do you do with this story? Interpret the story literally; what does it mean? Interpret it as symbolic and there also, is truth.

Sure, he could calm the storm? Back at the very beginning of these studies, the introduction of John claims divinity for Jesus. John 1:1-3: "in the beginning was the Word, and the Word was with God, and the Word was God. He was with God in the **beginning. Through him all thing was made; without him nothing was made that has been made."** Verse 14; "And the Word became flesh and made his dwelling among us." That being so, why can he who made all things not control all things. The argument is simple. But was there another teaching for the disciples. You decide. It was and is not unusual for storms to be used as metaphor. The poet, musicians of the Old Testament painted word pictures in the Psalms. Some entail storms as metaphor: Psalm 46:1-3, "God is our refuge and strength, an ever-present help in trouble.

Therefore we will not fear, though the earth gives way and the mountains fall into the heart of the surging sea." See also Psalm 107:23-32.

Did Jesus use the storm as a teaching tool? The meaning could sound like this. "Listen, I am in a storm of trouble." The religious leaders are closing in on me like a hurricane. You have not seen anything yet. But all is well with my mission. It is on course. I am greater than the storm. There is life beyond the storm." In coming lessons Jesus will tell them plainly that he is going to Jerusalem and will die there at the hands of ignorant men. Jesus rebuke to the disciples is that after all they had seen and heard they still lacked faith and understanding.

Application to Life

Taken literally and metaphorically there is an ongoing call to have faith in Jesus in the storms of life. You could sing or read the words of an old gospel song by Cantingly. When the storms of life are raging stand by me. When the world is tossing me, like a ship upon the sea Thou who rules wind and water, Stand by me. In the midst of fault and failures, stand by me. When I do the best I can, and my friends don't understand Thou who knows all about me, stand by me. Or sing and discuss:

Master the tempest is raging, the billows ore tossing high! The sky is over shadowed with blackness, no shelter or help is nigh: Carets thou not that we perish? How canst thou lie asleep, when each moment so madly is threatening a grave in the angry deep. Master with anguish of spirit I bow in my grief today. The depths of my sad heart are troubled; O waken and save, I pray. Torrents of sin and of anguish sweep o'er my sinking soul! And I perish! I perish, dear Master; O hasten and take control!" -Mary Baker

Did you ever feel as the hymn writers? Both in the Bible, Old and New Testaments, and to this day persons cry out to God in distress of the storms of life.

Jesus Healed the Gerasene Demoniacs
Matthew 8:28-34; Mark 5:1-20; Luke 8:26-39

In an earlier study, Jesus Healed a Demoniac in the Synagogue, Mark 1:21-28. The setting for this study is a cemetery in a rural area of Gennesaret; a town on the northwest shore of the Sea of Galilee. Jesus and his disciples had crossed to the shore and as they got out of the boat there was loud noise. A shout was heard, "What do you want with us, Son of God? Have you come to torture us before the appointed time?" Matthew 8:29. You may debate the meaning of being possessed by devils or demons. Many of the symptoms told in the story mimic what today would be called mental illness and/ or personality disorders. Uncontrolled wildness and emotions are felt and expressed. Note that Matthew said there were two men. Mark and Luke said one man. Suggestions for this study are centered in the men's demoniac **symptoms**; Jesus gave the men **signs** of wholeness; and the story had **symbolic** meaning.

The men had demoniac symptoms. Consider five. Could their nakedness indicate their lack of care for other people and themselves? Was it a sign of utter lack of value for themselves? They had no home. Living? Existing among the graves; was this an indication of their rejection of society and society's rejection of them. Their self-depreciation was depicted by the way they cut and harmed themselves. Though strong enough to break chains they were filled with fear. Fear of what was to come? Paranoia? They may have felt in control but were controlled by powers beyond themselves.

Jesus cast out the demons and gave the men signs of wholeness. And he sent the demons into a herd of swine. The hogs ran down into the sea and drowned. The pig herders ran into town to tell what had happened. Matthew said the whole town came out to see. There are times when you may see humor during the most serious events. This is one of those times. The town people came to the grave yard and there sat two men who had been naked, wild, uncontrollable. But now they were sitting, clothed and in their right minds. And the people were afraid! They beg Jesus to leave their country. Who was possessed by what then? Change is scary. Why not leave those guys alone in the cemetery? Is that what often happens? Some say grief led to their condition.

Two other signs of wholeness were their desire to follow Jesus and their obedience; going home and telling what God had done for them. Jesus later returned to Gennesaret. "When they had crossed over, they landed at Gennesaret....as soon as they got out of the boat, people recognized Jesus." Read Mark 6:53-56 and see if you think the crowd was there because these men had told the good news.

There are at least two things to consider. Did you know that the pig or hog was the mascot for the soldiers stationed in Jerusalem? Why else, then that Jews were forbidden to eat pork? The whole herd of pigs drowned in the sea. Does that suggest anything to you about the future of Rome?

The second idea has to do with Matthew making a lot of comparisons of Jesus to Moses. Do you know the Old Testament story of Moses leading the children of Israel out of Egypt? The water of Red or Reed Sea parted, and Moses and his people walked through on dry ground. Then the pursuing Egyptian army bogs down in the bed of the sea, the waters return and drowned them. So, is Matthew saying that like Moses, he symbolically drowned the enemy?

Application to Life

Aa major question to answer is: Who are the people who are outcasts in your society? What can you or your group do to help bring wholeness and acceptance to those persons?

Discuss the characteristics of wholeness (salvation) mentioned above and add to the list. Does salvation have to do with becoming a whole person here and now?

Who are the people of whom you are afraid? Why? What can you do to not fear?

List issues such as mental illness that you should take a positive stand to change. Jesus saw all persons as valuable, created in God's image. Do you?

Jesus Healed the Woman with an Issue of Blood
Matthew 9:20-22; Mark 5:21-34; Luke 8:43-48

This Bible passages for this study and the one to follow should be read together. The next study will be: Jesus Raised Jairus' Daughter from the Dead (Matthew 9:18-26; Mark 5:21-43; Luke 8:40-56). So please, stop now and read the stories of both events.

You saw that one story interrupts the other story. Then the other story continues. Some call of this type story telling "book ends;" others "sandwich."

Both stories have some very strong similarities and contrasts. Similarities: both the synagogue leader or ruler, Jairus, and the unnamed lady need help; both were desperate; both came to Jesus for help. Contrasts: a male with power, prestige and possessions; a female who lacks all three; he a ruler of the place of worship; she banned from the synagogue because of her physical condition Read Leviticus 15:19-32 for a description of how life was for a lady with normal and abnormal hemorrhaging. Whatever possessions this lady had were gone; paid to doctors. She was not better after twelve years. Luke and Mark agreed on that much. Mark, but not physician Luke, said she had gotten worse.

For this study concentrate on these two people and the courageous choices they made. The next study will concentrate on Jesus and the courageous choices he made regarding Jairus and the unnamed suffering lady. The courage to make right choices is the key idea in both studies. Life is made of choices. Choices determine destiny.

The Synagogue Ruler came to Jesus in an emergency. He was desperate. His only daughter, twelve years old, was dying. She was at the point of death. Matthew had him saying "My daughter has just died" verse 18. What leaves one with a more helpless feeling than the near-death illness or death of a child? In the first study of Part 3 of this Story of Jesus, a nobleman had a son who died. Jesus raised him from the dead, John 4:46-54. The fact that it was a daughter in a male dominated society does not seem to matter to the father. He is desperate. Little girls are valuable beyond words to describe.

It took courage for the ruler of the synagogue to come to Jesus. He had to know that Jesus was being watched by higher religious leaders than him. Some Jerusalem leaders were out to get Jesus. The choice to go to Jesus may have been dangerous personally and professionally. He came to Jesus anyway. He fell before Jesus pleading for him to come and save his daughter's life. She was twelve years old. That is the age of Bat Mitzvah. Mitzvah means commandment. So, daughter of the commandment.

As you know from reading the Bible passage, Jesus went to his home and raised the daughter to life. She walked around, and Jesus said to give her something to eat. How down to earth can you get? And is there a greater miracle than giving life?

The woman came to Jesus in exhaustion, desperation and probably very poor. For twelve years the lady in the story had suffered from hemorrhages. By religious laws he was unclean and contagious. She had suffered physically, psychologically, socially and spiritually. She had suffered for as many years as Jairus daughter had lived.

Speaking of choices of courage, how many rules, civil and religious, do you think the lady broke by choosing to come to Jesus? No doubt she knew she was breaking them. Even being in the crowd she was out of place. Touching Jesus, a male and the attraction of the crowd took some courage.

She was desperate and exhausted. Can you imagine being in her condition? Besides, she had been to how many doctors? She had spent all her money. She was not better but had grown worse. She must have been dead tired. She made her choice. She thought "If I just touch his clothes, I will be healed" (Mark 5:28). She did, and she was healed. Jesus recognized power had gone from him. When she realized that Jesus knew she was the one who touched him, she fell at his feet. He pronounced her clean. He said, "Your faith has healed you" Mark 5:34. And what faith she had and acted upon.

Application to Life

You do not have to wait until you have an emergency or are exhausted to come to Jesus. Think briefly about bad and good choices you have made and their consequences. How do you make right choices? What must be considered? You may want to consider studying *Choices: Making Right Decisions in a Complex World* by Lewis B. Smedes. Pray for wisdom to make right choices.

Jesus Raised Jairus' Daughter from the Dead
Matthew 9:18-26; Mark 5:21-43; Luke 8:40-56

This lesson and the previous one go together. One story interrupts another story. In the previous study the faith and courage of Jairus and the woman with the hemorrhage were discussed. Both took real risks in going to see Jesus. Jairus could have had religious and professional fears because he was a leader in the synagogue. Some, with higher religious authority and positions, were very much against Jesus. The woman was breaking religious and civil law just to be with the crowd, much less touch a man, Jesus. Jairus' twelve-year-old daughter was resuscitated, and the woman had her hemorrhage cured by Jesus. This study deals with the courage, compassion and sensitivity of Jesus.

Jesus was in constant danger from some of the Jewish religious leaders. Jesus was not the type Messiah (Christ) they were expecting or wanted. Jesus came in nonviolent love to show the WAY to peace and the common good. All the empires from Egypt, Assyria, Babylon, Persia, and now Rome believed in and practiced "peace" through violence. Do as Empire say or else…prison or crucifixion. This was the Roman way. Not many lessons after this one, other religious leaders, called Sadducees, will also be after Jesus. When Jesus recognized that the woman had touched him, he let it be known. The woman knew that Jesus knew, and she fell before him, confessed what she had done. With courage Jesus said, "Daughter, your faith has healed you. Go in peace" (Luke 8:48).

Was it not courageous of Jesus to go home with the leader of the synagogue? He had already experienced a lot of criticism for what he did. Could this have been a "trap" set by them to get him away from the crowd? Did they desired to get him alone and question him in private to find reason to arrest him?

Compassion is a feeling for and with those who hurt. It is the deep desire to relieve their suffering. Or just to be with them in their pain and grief. There are twenty-four studies in this Part 3, called Jesus' Great Galilean Ministry. One half of the studies deal with Jesus healing. In two he raised persons to life from death. Persons were primary in Jesus ministry. He cared, and he acted. Race, religion, sex, nationality were not barriers to Jesus' compassion. Every person, regardless, is a child of God and of utmost value.

How embarrassing do you think it was for this "unclean" woman to be found out by the crowd? Imagine her feelings of self-worthlessness. How could she face these people when and if she got to return to the synagogue? How did Jesus show sensitivity to her?

Now switch roles and consider how Jesus was sensitive to Jairus. About the time that Jesus told the woman to go in peace, word arrived that the little girl was dead. "Hearing this, Jesus said to Jairus, 'Don't be afraid; just believe, and she will be healed.'" (Luke 8:50). When they got to Jairus' house, Jesus only allowed three of his disciples to go in. They were Peter, James, and John. The only others that went into the girl's room where her father and mother. Jesus not only kept others out, he ordered them to stop the wailing. He told them that she was not dead but sleeping. They laughed at him. Then in the quietness of her room, Jesus took the little girl by the hand and said, "My child, get up" (Luke 8:54). He gave her to her parents and suggested they get her something to eat. How practical and sensitive can you get? Jesus was not there for praise or recognition.

There was a 'now' in the work of Jesus. In all the healings of the Galilean ministry Jesus was urgent about now. The Kingdom is here. It is about caring for the uncared for; about healing, feeding and justice. It is important to do the work of God now; to show the love of God now. Courage, compassion, and sensitivity are present needs. Living the life of love is to be done now. Jesus words were, 'Follow me."

Application to Life

Review some of the previous lessons and note how the healed ones acted immediately. Peter's mother in law, cured of her fever, got up and served. The demoniac went home and told what great things God had done for him.

When was a time you showed courage to stand for the right? When was a time you showed compassion? Recall a recent time you were sensitive to the needs of another.

Think about and discuss how you can show these characteristics NOW.

Jesus Healed Two Blind Men and A Man Who Was Mute
Matthew 9:27-34; 13:54-58; Mark 6:1-6

The story for this study is in the Matthew 9 passage. Matthew 13 and Mark 6passages indicate the time and place of the healing. Jesus Great Galilean Ministry was ending. In the next study Jesus sends his disciples twelve to do what he was doing: proclaiming the Kingdom of God is at hand; healing the sick; raising the dead; and casting out evil spirits.

Earlier in this Galilean ministry Jesus had healed a man who was blind and mute (Matthew 12:22-45; Mark 3:19-30). In that lesson the emphasis was made that Jesus literally healed the man. He could see and speak. But the healing carried a strong symbolic message. The people were not "seeing" Jesus, nonviolent, as Christ. They were amazed at his teaching and astounded by his miracles but could not grasp the idea that he came to save the world through nonviolent love.

In this lesson, many days, miracles and teachings later, Jesus performed the same miracles. This time Matthew said there were two blind men. Could this relate to Old Testament law, that required two witnesses to prove a truth or convict an accused? Could there be a second chance kind of emphasis? "You did not see (get it) the first time and you still do not see." After all he had done, they still did not see.

In the first story the blind man was brought to Jesus and he healed him. Brief and to the point. In this story two blind men were following and calling out to Jesus. Jesus went into a house before responding to the men. Was he trying to get privacy for the miracle? Jesus asked them if they believed he could heal them. They responded, yes. Jesus said that their healing would be according to their faith. There is no question that faith in God is a plus in the healing process today. But there is real danger of disappointment when people think that you just have faith and God will heal.

There are many factors that enter the causes of diseases and the healing ministry. Jesus also healed the man who could not speak. "He was brought to Jesus." The cause of his muteness was attributed to evil spirits, which Jesus drove out. Today this would probably be considered a psychosomatic disease.

A person can see and not understand. A person can speak and speak untruth; as did Jesus' critics. A person can refuse to speak when he should speak out.

What were the people, both followers and critics, failing to see? Go back and read once again Luke 4:14-30. Jesus came to his home synagogue and read from Isaiah the prophet. Having read, he sat to teach, He said that on this very day this prophesy was being fulfilled. The Kingdom of God was near. He would "preach good news to the poor…. proclaim freedom for the prisoners and recovery of sight for the blind, release the oppressed, proclaim the year of the Lord's favor." That sounded great until he inferred that this was for all people. Then, they were ready to kill him.

It would be good at this point, whether you are studying alone or in a group, to read some related Old Testament passages about the hoped-for Messiah and the Kingdom of God. "In that day the deaf will hear the words of the scroll, and out of gloom and darkness the eyes of the blind will see" Isaiah 29:18. "Then will the eyes of the blind be opened and the ears of the deaf unstopped. Then the lame will leap like a deer, and the mute tongue shout for joy" Isaiah 35:5-6. Isaiah 42:18-19 tells of people like Jesus encountered. They had ears but would not hear. Psalm 146 also gives a good description of the work of God. Trust is him not in weapons of war, it says.

Application to Life

Ponder the greatness of God's love for all people as revealed in the life and teachings of Jesus. Do you think the wonder drugs and surgeries along with all the wonderful discoveries to aid healing are a gift of God? Are they meant for all people or a "lucky" few? How do pride, greed and consumption fit into the picture you have of Jesus? If the Kingdom of God is here and now, as well as future, should more attention be given to seeing that all people have the basics of life? How does following Jesus relate to what we do for those around us?

Jesus Sent Out Seventy Disciples
Matthew 9:35-38; 10:1-42; 11:1;
Mark 6:6-13; Luke 10:1-24

This is the last of twenty-four studies on Jesus' Great Galilean Ministry. In this study Jesus sent out his twelve disciples. He gave them authority to do what he had been doing. They were to preach the kingdom of God, heal the sick, drive out demons, and according to Matthew even raise the dead. Matthew also notes that they were to go only to Jewish communities. Why? Could it be that they are the ones who should understand the Messiah? He wanted them to know that God loved them, and they should recognize him as Messiah? He instructed them how they should live. He warned them of danger. He told them to trust in God.

They were to preach the kingdom of God is at hand. An earlier study suggested that the kingdom of God was defined in the prayer Jesus taught his disciples. "your kingdom come, your will be done on earth as it is in heaven" Matthew 6:10. This is not a new concept. For a brief idea of God as King of a kingdom read Psalm 96.

In Genesis 12, God told Abram (Abraham) that he would bless him and make him a great nation. Through that nation all the nations of the earth would be blessed or bless themselves. Blessing was given by God to be shared. Abraham's son, Isaac, received that same promise as did his son, Jacob. The sons of Jacob (Israel)were living in Egypt at the end of Genesis. The Book of Exodus begins with the children of Israel as slaves in Egypt (four hundred years later) crying out to God. God sends Moses and miraculously delivers them, with promises conditioned on their obedience to him. See Exodus chapter 20. Eventually a mighty empire or kingdom is established by King David. David receives promises from God that there would be one on his throne forever. The story of Solomon, son of David, is the story of an empire gone bad. The kingdom of Israel was divided. The northern kingdom retaining the name Israel fell to the empire, Assyria in 722 B.C. The southern kingdom called Judah, capital Jerusalem, fell to Babylon in 586 B.C.. Many of those exiled to

69Babylon returned about 50 years later. But the glory days of David's kingdom were never reached. The hope of the Jewish people in Jesus time was for a Messiah to come and deliver them from Roman anarchy. Here is the problem. God's kingdom is to be and always was to be a kingdom based on justice, mercy, freedom for all people. How opposite from peace brought about by war and violence. Knowing this story is essential to understand Jesus mission and the peoples' misunderstanding of it.

No swords, no implements of war, but healing, compassion, and love is what Jesus lived and taught. That is what the disciples were sent to proclaim. God loves all people!

Instruction for what to carry and not carry on the mission was to live simply. Depend on hosts, take no pay. Saint Frances took this literally. Simple living is a hard lesson for people who are driven by capitalism and consumerism.

If the teacher, Jesus, had been persecuted, so would the pupils. It is not popular to proclaim a gospel that disturbs the religious leaders. The Old Testament prophets learned that the hard way. Their message was that God did not want sacrifices, but right living. The two major sins then and now are idolatry and social injustice. Whenever something or someone takes the place of God in your life, that is idolatry. Whenever anyone is treated with injustice it is social injustice.

They were not to worry when brought before the court. The Spirit of God was there and as teacher, would give them words. As a saint said long ago, it isn't that Christianity has been tried and failed, it has not been tried.

Application to Life

Think about how present-day empires compare to the Roman Empire. Rule by might. Who has the biggest and most bombs? How much budget is spent on war machines, as compared to education, jobs, health care, essentials available for all? How should followers of Jesus live in such a world or empire?

Part 4

Jesus Trained His Twelve Disciples

Jesus Fed More Than 5,000 People
Matthew 14:13-21; Mark 6:30-44; Luke 9:10-17; John 6:1-13

This study is the first of nine that Dr. Robertson labeled, "Jesus taught his 12 disciples." Therefore, each study will attempt to discover what the disciples should or could have learned from being with, listening to and watching Jesus.

The setting had two back ground stories. One, the disciples had returned from their mission elated with their success. Second, Jesus had just heard that John the Baptist had been killed by Herod. Jesus saw this as a time for a retreat.

He got into a boat to start across the Lake of Galilee toward Bethsaida. The crowd saw him and raced to Bethsaida on foot. Jesus knew of a deserted place for contemplating, teaching, prayer and rest. Jerusalem and crucifixion lay ahead. Jesus had led the disciples to a mountain side when he saw the crowd following. He had compassion on them. He changed his plans and taught the crowd and healed the sick. Late in the day he and the disciples knew that the crowd was tired and hungry. The disciples told Jesus to send them away, so they could buy food for themselves. Jesus told the disciples to feed the crowd. Pick up with John's version of the story. He said Phillip told Jesus it would take 200 days wages to buy the crowd a snack. Andrew had been observing the crowd and told Jesus that a boy was there with a lunch. The lunch had 5 barley loaves and 2 small fish. But Andrew doubted that would help with so many to feed.

Jesus had the disciples to put the people in groups of 50 and 100 and have them sit on the grass. Jesus blessed, broke and gave the bread and fish, to the disciples to serve the people. All ate and were filled. There were 12 baskets of leftovers.

For many the story is taken at face value. Why not? Jesus had power to take the small lunch and multiply it endlessly. By the way, the blessing of the bread may have been a Jewish prayer: "Blessed are you O Lord our God, King of the universe who brings forth bread from the ground." A story tells that when the Israelites, who had eaten manna that fell from heaven for years in the desert (Exodus), got to the promise land and saw grain growing from the ground, this prayer was prayed. They saw "bread from the ground" as a miracle of God.

Some think another miracle may have taken place. The power of influence; one boy shared his lunch and all who had food with them began to share. A miracle of community is important. That is worth thinking about.

A problem arose. Some of the people wanted to declare Jesus as their King. He rejected the idea. He knew some were only interested in the free bread. Does this remind you of Jesus temptations in the wilderness, Matthew chapter 3?

What did Jesus' disciples learn? Here are a few suggestions:

Heading the list is compassion. Jesus had compassion on the people. Compassion is at the heart of major religions. Do you think trust is a major teaching? The disciples were challenged to feed the people. Jesus knew what he was going to do. He wanted them to trust him. Remember why they had gone across the lake? Physical and spiritual retreat. Patience with interruptions surely is a lesson needed then and now. Jesus had it. The boy taught a lesson in sharing. What do you have that needs sharing?

Application to Life

Try to list as least five more lessons from this study. One might be, do not waste. Think on which of these lessons you do well and how you can improve on one that gives you problems. Oh, forgot, this is the only miracle told in all four gospels. You may want to memorize the Jewish prayer and say it before meals. Later in John 6:35 Jesus said, "I am the bread of life." Do you think he meant that whoever followed him, and his way of living would find life at its fullest?

Jesus Walked on the Water
Matthew 14:22-36; Mark 6:45-56; John 6:14-21

After he fed the 5,000 (Matthew 14:13-21), Jesus went onto the mountain to pray. He sent his disciples away by boat so that he could be alone. During the night a ferocious wind came up and the disciples were afraid. It was early between 3 and 6 in the morning that they all saw Jesus coming toward them, walking on the water. Then, they became terrified. They thought they were seeing a ghost.

It has been suggested that the gospel writers have depicted Jesus as a new Moses. If you watch, you will see comparisons between Jesus and Moses. This is one of them. And in this study, there will be more. But to illustrate; in Exodus 3:7-8, God said to Moses "I have indeed **seen** the misery of my people in Egypt. I have **heard** them crying out because of their slave drivers, ….so I am **come down** to deliver…" Now, note in the passages for this study; Jesus **saw** the disciples struggling in the storm. He **came** to them. He **calmed the wind.** Or you can think of the water of the Red Sea parting, and Moses and his people crossing on dry ground. Jesus simply walked on the water. For this study, think of Jesus as the Bread of life.

Do not get caught up in arguments about how or did Jesus walk on water, and miss the truth in the story, which is of all things, about **BREAD.** This is not to say there are no other lessons in the study. But look at Mark 6:52: "for they had not understood about the loaves; their hearts were hardened." What about the loaves? Right, Jesus had just provided bread for 5,000 plus, with twelve baskets left over. How does that relate to this story?

As part of the furnishings for the tabernacle or tent of meeting, there was to be a table for the **bread of the presence**. Did not the bread represent the presence of God? Now go back to John 6:35 where Jesus said, "I am the bread of life." God is present in Jesus. Matthew 1:23 says he would be called Emmanuel, which means God is with us. In Matthew 28:20, the last verse of the book, Jesus said, "I am with you always, even to the end of the age." The one-point lesson for this study is that God is always **present** with and in his people

Recall the temptation experience in Matthew 4:4, Jesus said, "Man does not live on bread alone, but on every word that comes from the mouth of God. John chapter one, Jesus is the living Word, creator, who became flesh. He was present for the disciples in the boat. Their problem was lack of trust in his presence. Therefore, the Eucharist or Lord's Supper is so important. The eating of the bread is symbolic of the body of Christ. The idea is that the presence of God is in the bread and thus in you. The metaphor of life sustaining bread is a powerful reminder that God is always with you. The question for the study, had the disciples not under stood that the bread represented the ever-present God with them? Had they forgotten another storm experience when Jesus was with them and they were afraid? They needed to have faith that God knows, cares and is present in the good times and the bad.

Where can I go from your Spirit?
Where can I flee from your presence?
If I go up to heaven, you are there.
If I make my bed in Sheol, you are there.
If I rise on the wings of the dawn,
if I settle on the far side of the sea
even there your hand shall guide me
your right hand will hold me fast. Psalm 139:7-10

Application to Life

Read and meditate on Psalm 139:1-18. This is how close God is to you. Does the

Psalm not make you grateful for such a present, caring and delivering God? List other lessons from this story, such as trust, obedience, and Peter's doubt. Why do you think Jesus was going to go past them? Why did Peter fail his water walk? Would this be a good time for you and your group to observe the Lord's Supper? Remember the present studies are about Jesus training the 12 disciples. What do you think they learned? What did you learn? Learning means change in knowledge, attitude or action? What change will you practice today or this week?

Jesus Did Not Conform to People's Expectations
Matthew 15:1-20; Mark 7:1-23;
John 6:22-71; 7:1

This study combines parallel stories from Matthew and Mark with a different story from John. All three stories emphasize the conflicts Jesus had with some of the Jewish religious leaders. Jesus was not conforming to their expectations of the Christ. Keep in mind, Jesus was a Jew by race, religion and residence. He was **not** trying to begin a new religion. His mission was to show the people, including the leaders, that God loves all people. And the mission of Judaism was to so love and obey God that all nations would be blessed through them by seeing the love of God manifest in them.

Their expectation was for a Christ or Messiah who would be like King David. A warrior king who would overthrow their enemies, set them free and build an empire. Jesus turned their empire idea upside down. So, his enemies wanted to be rid of him.

In this study Jesus showed that religious traditions and power can bind and blind; that hypocrisy skews the reality within a person; and true-life giving bread is trusting and following the example and teachings of Jesus. It is a relationship of faith.

The problem in the Matthew and Mark passages has to do with observance a non-biblical tradition, not a command of God. The washing hands before meals and even during meals had to do with a ritual custom that had become a "tradition" of the elders. Traditions and the power to enforce them have been used by religious leaders for eons. This is a control factor. You must believe as I believe, or else. You must worship and practice rituals like my group or you are wrong. History is filled with this. This is one source of church "splits," witch hunting, crusades, and martyrs. Tradition and manmade rules are used to bind people to a way and blind them to new truths.

Hypocrisy relies on outward appearance; reality is in the heart, intent and being. Do you think Jesus may have been tired of the Pharisees constant accusations? To call someone a hypocrite is very strong language. The opposition is not going to let up. Jesus made it clear those religious people had blinded themselves to the truth.

Hand washing tradition had become a show thing. Look, I am religious. But Jesus 'challenge goes beyond that. He calls their attention to the fourth commandment: "Honor your father and your mother…" Jesus said that the accusers used another tradition in order to not obey this law which would call for caring for their parents in old age. The tradition, corban (dedicated to God), gave them a loophole. They could say their wealth was dedicated (like willed) to God so they did not have to use any of it to care for the needs of aging parents. BANG. Bet they were not expecting that. To drive that home, he said they did a lot of things like that.

Hypocrisy is mask wearing. It is wanting people to think you are something that you are not. Jesus concluded by teaching the disciples that what matters is inward, in the heart, not what you looked like outwardly. If the heart is right, right comes out. If it is evil, evil come out. Thoughts – words – deeds- habits- character – destiny.

Now to the John passage. Here again is that bread metaphor. Jesus is the bread. Bread is necessary for life. Jesus said in the passage that his flesh and blood were to be consumed. Knowing what you know about Jesus and common reason says this is metaphor. The idea is that you are to have such a faith relationship with Jesus that he is essential to your life and wellbeing. Have you not said or heard it said to a baby or small child, "I could eat you up." It means I love you with all my heart. When has someone told you, "I devoured that book? " They meant the same as "I could not put it down." The Eucharist – Lord's Supper is a symbol of this love and devotion to Christ.

Application to Life

Are there traditions in your life that have hindered you from searching for truth or believing new truth? When you encounter a stranger or new friend, do you listen to what they have to say as well as saying what you need to say?

Do you think that churches today have traditions? Name some. Can churches and persons be more concerned about a set of beliefs than following Jesus?

Are there times when you feel like a hypocrite? Why? How hard is it for you to really be just who you are? That is; your best self, of course?

You may want to express your love and thanksgiving for Jesus through prayer and song. Give thanks for his love: inclusive love; forgiving love, compassionate love...add to the list. Commit yourself to love him back by loving others. What do you think the disciples learned from these experiences? What did you learn? The next study is Jesus Healed the Daughter of a Siro-Phoenician Woman Matthew 15:21-28; and Mark 7:24-30.

Jesus Healed The Daughter Of A Syrian-Phoenician Woman
Matthew 15:21-28; Mark 7:24-30

Jesus had stopped another group of Jewish religious leaders who came from Jerusalem to accuse him Matthew 15:1-20. He left Capernaum with his disciples and retreated to the area of Tyre and Sidon. The retreat was not to hide because of fear. Jesus needed privacy to rest, pray and teach his disciples. They still did not understand enough about Jesus and his mission. You may recall how retreats around Lake Galilee had been interrupted by the crowds. This time he led the disciples west toward the Mediterranean Sea. He went into non-Jewish territory.

But word about him had spread that way also. A Syrian-Phoenician woman heard about Jesus and found him. Under Roman rule the two countries had been combined. The woman is called a Greek or Gentile, she was called a Canaanite, the name of the early settlers of the whole region, including Israel.

This woman followed Jesus, crying out, "Lord, Son of David, have mercy on me! My daughter is suffering terribly from demon-possession" Matthew 15:22. That really upset the disciples and they urged Jesus to send her away. But Jesus allowed her to follow and then he confronted her and granted her request.

Jesus refused to send her away, but his conversation with her was unusual. He said to her and/or to the disciples," I was sent only to the lost sheep of Israel" Matthew 15:24. What do you say to that? Does that sound like Jesus? In Mark 7:27,

Jesus said, "First, let the children eat all they want, for it is not right to take the children's bread and toss it to their dogs." WOW! What is going on? Jesus loved everyone, came to save the whole world. What does this mean? Here is a suggestion or two. First, Matthew is writing for Jews and/or Jewish Christians 40 years after this event. Jesus' mission was to the Jews first. They needed to understand that God, whom they had worshipped for hundreds of years, had chosen them to witness by word and deed about their God to the whole world. Instead of inclusive, they had become exclusive. Many of them had accepted the privilege without the responsibility. They were to have been a kingdom of priests to the whole world. Jesus came to show them a message they had forgotten.

Second idea could Jesus have been testing this woman's faith. Did she really believe him to be the Son of David? Did she really believe that he could heal her daughter? Son of David is a title for the Messiah or Christ, the one who was to come and deliver Israel. Again, be reminded that Jesus did not fit the mold of an expected military king. He was nonviolent to the end. His message and way were love is stronger than hate. Restoration is better than retribution. Redemption is better than recrimination.

In the second exchange of words, was Jesus introducing humor into the conversation? Perhaps he was. You decide. "It is not right to take the children's bread and toss it to their dogs," Jesus said. Was he calling the woman a dog? Was there a grin on Jesus face as he said that? What do you think? The woman is quick to match wits with him. "Yes, Lord, but even the dogs under the table eat the children's crumbs," she said. What an answer! Jesus must have loved this woman. It may have been the first laugh either of them had in a while. Humor is healing.

For such a reply, "You may go; the demon has left your daughter," Jesus said. Did you notice how the woman approached Jesus? Following, crying out her need, falling before him, and calling out his title, Son of David, Lord. What a picture of trouble and humility. Her hope was in finding Jesus. How would you describe her exit? You think she was smiling, maybe laughing? Do you think she was confident that what Jesus had said about her daughter was true? She certainly found it to be true when she got home.

Note some commonalities from the story. Mothers' love must be universal. It crosses every kind of boundary and barrier: race, religion, nationality, color, or whatever. Mothers' love may be about the closest thing mankind has to God's love. Disease and evil are also everywhere and attack all manner of people.

Application to Life

How many persons of another race, nationality or religion do you know? How many consider you a friend? What are major barriers in your society to accepting others as equal? Think of ways you can meet and befriend such persons. Do they know that you are a follower of Jesus? Would they be welcome in your home and church? Are you a follower of Jesus? Like the woman in the story, you can fall before him and ask for his mercy and decide now to follow him.

Jesus Healed a Deaf Man and Fed More than 4,000 People
Matthew 15:29-38; Mark 7:31-37; 8:1-9

In the last study from Matthew 15:21-28 and Mark 7:24-30, Jesus had gone on retreat away from Capernaum, familiar Galilean territory. He had gone to gentile territory near or in Tyre. There he had healed a Syrian-Phoenician woman's daughter. In familiar territory the crowd had gotten to his retreat area before he and the disciples got there. He needed time and privacy to teach the disciples, pray and prepare for what lay ahead. We are not told how long he stayed in Tyre, but leaving there he went to Sidon, some thirty miles to the north.

By the way, it is worth your time to stop and read about Ahab, King of Israel (northern kingdom), marrying Jezebel. She was the daughter of the king of Sidon. She was a worshipper of the Canaanite god, Baal. She and Ahab led many in Israel to worship Baal. Then Elijah showed up to announce God's displeasure expressed in a long drought. Elijah went to Zarephath, nearby and raised a widow's son to life.

Why connect this to the study? In lesson 8 there is reference to Elijah. Do you think Jesus, who does so many things like Elijah that some think he is Elijah resurrected, would want to see the place or area where Elijah had worked? Back to Sidon. The passages do not tell us how long Jesus stayed. From there he went to the area on the east of Lake Galilee called Decapolis. Decapolis means ten cities. The time period of this retreat may have been weeks. Somewhere in this area crowd gathered and spent three days with Jesus as he taught and healed. He was still in gentile country. Among those healed was a deaf man. Then he fed 4,000 or more.

The deaf man also had a speech impediment. The is unique, the only time Jesus had to make two attempts to get the healing done. Or is that the point of the lesson? Recall, there were other deaf and mute healings (Matthew 12:22 and 9:32). The healings are real, but they are also metaphorical truth. The deaf cannot or will not hear. It took multiple times for Jesus to get the truth to his disciples so that they would speak correctly about him and his mission. Matthew 15:31 says that the people "praised the God of Israel." That is the point. The acts and teaching of Jesus pointed people to the God of Israel, who is God of the whole wide world.

Some think this is a repeat telling of feeding the 5,000. But here the place is not near Capernaum. The people are different. The number is different. Dr. Wm. Barclay, noted New Testament scholar, wrote that the baskets are different. Interesting. The word for basket in the 5,000 story is a personal, small basket. The word in the 4,000 story is for a large basket, maybe by comparison, huge. Baskets differed in number.

Do the stories mean the same? What do you think? Was Jesus on this whole retreat making a point that the gospel is for all people? Was he showing that he is concerned about the needs of other peoples as well as Jews? Was that a lesson for the disciples to begin to learn? Take a moment and read the last two verses in Matthew 28.

If later you study the book of Acts, you will see this pattern being carried out by the disciples. The same pattern Jesus was using, good news to the Jews, then to everyone. In Acts, Paul often went first to the Synagogue in the towns where he preached.

Keep in mind, Eucharist or Lord's Supper may be inferred in these feeding stories. Jesus cared very much for the physical needs and met them, but the bread also symbolized his body given for us all. The leftover baskets symbolize the abundance of the bread of life. There is enough and to spare. There is love, grace, forgiveness for all. It is for you. That is good news. Have you decided to follow Jesus?

Application to Life

Think about the wonderful healing sources of modern time. Do you see them as a gift from God, Does God work through the many vocations of medicine? What about work in the prevention of diseases? Do you know your local statistics of hungry and diseased children and adults? What are you and your church doing to meet those needs? There are organizations that seek to provide food and clean water in underdeveloped nations as well as more developed nations.

Can we become so heavenly minded that we are no earthly good? Recall Jesus taught his disciples to pray; "Thy kingdom come, thy will be done **on earth** as it is in heaven."

Jesus Healed a Blind Man in Bethsaida
Matthew 15:39; 16:1-12; Mark 8:10-26

It would be good to read the preceding stories, starting with Matthew 14:13 and Mark 6:30. You will see that Jesus and his disciples were on retreat or attempting to be on retreat. Jesus needed time to pray, teach the disciples and prepare for what lay ahead. Jesus began near Capernaum, then to gentile territories of Tyre and Sidon, to the northwest and to Decapolis (10 cities) to the east of the Sea of Galilee. They crossed the Sea of Galilee twice. This study was in Magadan on the west shore of the Sea of Galilee and Bethsaida (house of fish) on the northeast shore of the sea.

Jesus again faced opposition. But the opposition had increased to include Sadducees and Herodians. You may not have heard of these Jewish sects, so take a moment and learn a few basics about each. **Pharisees** (separated ones) were lay persons who tried to keep Moses' law and the traditions that grew from them, some 613. They believed in afterlife and resurrection from the dead. **Sadducees** were aristocrats, connected to temple life and service. They supported the Roman power and status quo. They accepted only Moses law and did not believe in the resurrection, angels, or demons. A way to remember them: they denied the resurrection, so they were sad u see. Little is known about the **Herodians**. They were supporters of Herod and Rome. **Zealots** were a group of Jews who "carried a dagger" for Romans and their supporters. You may recall Jesus had a disciple, Matthew (writer of the gospel), a tax collector, and so, he worked for Rome. He also had a disciple called Simon the Zealot.

Back to today's study. Matthew said the Pharisees and Sadducees asked a sign from Jesus. "Politics and religion make strange bedfellows." The disciples still don't understand about leaven and bread. Jesus illustrated that by healing a blind man.

Pharisees asked for a sign. If they had not seen, they had heard of miraculous healings and the feeding of multitudes by multiplying bread and fish. They came to trap Jesus. He refused to participate in their game. Instead, Jesus reminded them that they could tell the weather signs. Why could they not interpret the signs that Jesus had done? Was Jesus accusing them of blindness to the works of God? They knew the scripture (Hebrew Bible or Old Testament). Why could they not see that Jesus was the Messiah predicted by Moses?

What was the sign of Jonah, referred to in the discussion? Jonah's three days in the big fish (Book of Jonah in the Old Testament) is a sign that Jesus would be in the grave three days. But, could it not also refer to the fact that the people of Nineveh heard Jonah preach the word of God, repented and were saved from impending disaster? And could the sign mean that God loves all people, even those who may be your enemy?

Jesus and his disciples set sail toward Bethsaida after the above encounter. On arriving the disciples realized they had but one loaf of bread in the boat. Matthew said they had no bread. This concern was prompted by a statement of Jesus. He warned them to beware of the leaven of the Pharisees and Sadducees. Jesus meant the teachings of those sects. The disciples thought of bread. Jesus knew their thoughts and scolded them for their lack of understanding. In their hunger, had they forgotten the events and meaning of Jesus feeding thousands? They needed to be careful about their pride and the danger of compromised ethics and misuse of power. They needed to remember they were not above others, but servants to others. Why would Mark write that they had one loaf? Is it possible he was thinking, Jesus is with us? He is the bread of life. He is the only loaf they needed.

Jesus healed a blind man. What is new about this? What Jesus does is always new. Consider the tender compassion used with the man. He took him by the hand, led him out of the city. The first time, the healing is only partial. Lack of power? No! Think about the lesson. Who had eyes that did not see yet? The disciples. Who needed to see correctly in order to speak without impediment? The disciples. Do you see the power of the metaphor?

Application to Life

You may want to read more about the Jewish sects in a Bible Dictionary. They become very prominent in the rest of the Jesus

Story. Think about how good religion can go wrong when it becomes a means to control people. Discuss with a friend or group the danger involved when the state controls the church or church controls the state. Talk about the danger of pride and prestige in religion. Do not forget that relationship with Jesus is by faith, He is the bread of life and relationship of faith in him is partaking of that bread. Can or does the church create beliefs to control its members?

Jesus Taught His Disciples at Caesarea Philippi
Matthew 16:13-28; Mark 8:27-38; Luke 9:18-27

This is the seventh study in chronological order on, Jesus trained his disciples. He taught them about himself and his mission by word and deed. They had a difficult time understanding. Most of these seven studies deal with Jesus and the disciples on retreats, to get away for rest and teaching. Time had become a factor.

The retreat in this study is at Caesarea-Philippi. Philip, son of Herod the Great, named the city after himself and Tiberias Caesar. It had other names before that. It had been a place for the worship of Baal, a Canaanite god. There the Greeks worshipped Pan. It was located at Mt. Hermon, about 30 miles north of the Sea of Galilee.

The story in this study is very familiar to Bible students and preachers. It has many subjects for sermons and studies such as: ideas about Jesus; Peter; the rock; the church, first time mentioned; keys to the kingdom; gates of hades. For this study the focus is on the main character, Jesus. He is the subject. The purpose of the retreat was to teach the disciples in plain language who Jesus was and what lay ahead for him. He asked them what others thought; whom they believed him to be; and then told them what was going to happen to him and what it would require of them.

Some thought Jesus was Elijah returned as promised by the prophet Malachi 4:5. Jesus had done miracles like those of Elijah. Others thought Jesus was John the Baptist risen from the dead. Herod had put John in prison and then had him killed. Read this in Luke 9:7-9; Matthew 14:1-12 and Mark 6:14-29. Jesus talked like a prophet and did some things that Old Testament prophets did. It would be easy to see why some would think he was one of the prophets raised from the dead.

Jesus began the discussion by asking the disciples who they thought him to be. Peter was quick to give the correct answer, but as the study shows, he did not understand the meaning of the answer. He said, "You are the Christ, the Son of the living God" Mat. 16:16; "You are the Christ" Mark 8:29; "You are the Christ of God" Luke

9:20. Peter got it right. In fact, Jesus said the answer was a revelation from God to Peter. Christ is the Greek word, Messiah is the Hebrew word. They mean anointed one.

Jesus then told the disciples that he was going to Jerusalem. He would be betrayed; the Roman authorities would have him crucified. Peter was quick to say that can't happen. That was not his belief about the Christ. They still had the idea of a military king. Jesus was not that and was not going to be.

The titles, Christ and Son of God further complicated the situation. These were titles claimed by Caesar. He was said to be divine, son of god, savior of the world. So, Jesus was being called by titles that the emperor claimed.

Jesus said to Peter, "Get behind me Satan." Peter one moment spoke words of a revelation from God. The next he rejects the way of God. Here is the heart of the mystery. Jesus is a suffering, servant, savior. His way is that of compassion, love, healing and life giving. That's opposite of violence, control and oppression. To follow him is to take up your cross and follow. Christianity is a way of living. It is done in community, or church. One of few times the word church is used. It means "called out" as to a town meeting. Following Jesus is called the Way in the Book of Acts. The cross was an instrument of death, execution. If a person lives as Jesus calls her/him to live there will be opposition. As in Jesus day, pride, possessions and power (political, business, institution, church) cause those who have it to oppress and control those who are poor and lack these things. Christians are to meet the needs of such people.

Jesus will teach this same lesson at least two more times. It is debatable whether the disciples ever learned the lesson until after Jesus' resurrection.

Application to Life

Who do you say that Jesus is? And what do you mean by your answer? Jesus lived a life of justice and love. He was crucified for breaking traditions. His way of life was a threat to the power and position of some powerful religious and political leaders. They made false accusations about him. Can you think of times when you must decide to follow Jesus by taking a stand against political or civil injustice? Read as your prayer Saint Francis' prayer:

Lord make me an Instrument of your Peace. Where there is hatred, let me sow love. Where there is injury, pardon; Where there is doubt, faith; Where there is despair, hope; Where there is darkness, light; Where there is sadness, joy. O Divine Master, Grant that I may not so much seek to be consoled, as to console, to be understood, as to understand, to be loved, as to love, for it is in giving that we receive; It is in pardoning that we are pardoned; it is in dying that we are born to eternal life.

Jesus Was Transfigured
Matthew 17:1-113; Mark 9:1-13; Luke 9:28-36

Wonderful things happen on mountains. In this study Jesus was transfigured before three of his disciples. Within a few days of the last story, which was in Caesarea-Philippi, Jesus takes Peter, James and John onto a high mountain. Mark and Matthew said six days. Luke said about eight days. Many scholars think it was Mount Hermon, because it was only a few miles north of Caesarea-Philippi. It is a high mountain, 9,100 feet above sea level. The peaks could be seen from the Dead Sea over one hundred miles to the south.

Do not forget that Jesus had a lot of followers, including women. He had chosen 12 men, to whom he gave extra instruction and training. Of that twelve, there seemed to be an "inner circle," who got even more time with Jesus. These three have been and will be alone with Jesus at certain times (examples Mark 5:37 and 14:33). Special privilege meant special responsibility. The disciples saw Jesus transfigured, heard a voice, and received a command.

None of the stories said how high up the mountain they climbed. It must have been an exhausting trip. Luke indicates the three disciples were tired and may have fallen asleep. Jesus was praying. Luke said that they had gone there to pray. Jesus was transfigured before them. That got them wide awake. Not only was Jesus there, Moses and Elijah were there talking with Jesus. The word for transfigure means metamorphose, complete change. It is the butterfly idea of change. It is the same word Paul used in Romans 12:2, "be transformed by the renewing of your mind." The other time it is used is in 2 Corinthians 3:18, "we …. are being transformed into his likeness…."Could this have been a fore gleam of his resurrected body? Could the brilliance of his clothes and face remind them of Moses coming down the mountain; his face so reflected God's he had to cover it? Read this in Exodus 34:29-35.

Also present was Elijah, the great prophet, who would return according to the last verse in the book of Malachi. Jesus told them that John the Baptist fulfilled that prophecy.

The disciples were terrified. Would you not have been? Jesus told them not to be afraid. How many times has he had to tell them that?

The law giver, Moses, and the prophet Elijah talked with Jesus. "They spoke about his departure, which he was about to bring to fulfillment in Jerusalem" Luke 9:30-31. That sounds like his death, does it not?

A major teaching in these passages is that Jesus was and is the fulfillment of law and the prophets. Jesus was the live body living out the law and prophet. He is saying follow me in order to be and do what God desires as spoken by the law and the prophets. Did these disciples understand the drama any better than the words of Jesus? It is doubtful.

Peter had to say something. He suggested they put up three tabernacles. Did he recall the tabernacle in the Old Testament which represented the place of God for them? Luke said Peter did not know what he was saying. A cloud covered them. Often in the Old Testament a cloud represented the presence of God. It was a cloud that led the Israelites and Moses through the wilderness by day. A fire led them at night. So, there was metaphor for God's presence. A voice from the cloud told them that Jesus was the beloved Son of God. They were told to listen to him. This scene may cause you to think back to Jesus' baptism. Similar words were spoken there. Surely the event was to teach the disciples about Jesus and what lay ahead. But don't forget, Jesus was human. He knew that he was not only on "the most wanted" list but would be betrayed by one of his own and meet an early death. Try to imagine the pressure he is under. Do you think he ever had doubts that he could be wrong about his persistence on the Kingdom of God being one of love, peace, freedom and nonviolence? Could he have needed that word from God, "You are my beloved Son?"

Do not tell anyone about this until after the resurrection. Do you think they obeyed? Do you think they even understood yet that Jesus was going to die? It was surely encouraging for them to know and remember later. They also included the story in the gospels as a witness for those who read them then and now.

Application to Life

Give thought to how the whole Bible, Old Testament and New Testament, makes one story of God's revelation of himself, culminating in Jesus the Christ. The God of Moses is the God of Elijah, is the God of Jesus who calls us to follow him. Consider reading the story of Moses in Exodus. and Elijah's story in the book of I Kings. Does transformation, as Paul used it in the Romans and II Corinthian passages mean that following Jesus is a lifelong process of being transformed into God's intention for us?

Jesus Healed a Demoniac Boy
Matthew 17:14-20; Mark 9:14-29; Luke 9: 37-43

A crowd, including the left behind disciples and critics, awaited Jesus, Peter, James, and John when the four came down the mountain. They had experienced the glorious event of Jesus "transfiguration." Peter had suggested that three tents be erected for Jesus, Moses and Elijah. The inference is that Peter would like to have stayed on the mountain with the three celebrities (Matthew 17:1-13).

But they had to come down. This is often the experience in life. You have an extraordinary experience on retreat from everyday life, but you must return to everyday work. Jesus returned to a loud and confused crowd. There was arguing and discontent when Jesus got there. A man was shouting out for Jesus to heal his only son. The disciples had failed in their effort to heal the boy.

Jesus had come from the mountain where Moses and Elijah had appeared to him. Those two had similar experiences to this. Moses came down from Mount Sinai and found his people had rebelled and built an idol to worship (Exodus 32). Elijah came down from the victorious contest with the prophets of Baal on Mount Carmel and heard that Jezebel was planning to kill him (2 Kings 18 and 19).

In this study Jesus was disappointed with the lack of faith of the disciples. Jesus healed the boy. Jesus instructed his disciples.

Was Jesus frustrated, disappointed, grieved or all three and more? The crowd was confused, the disciples had failed to heal the boy, and the whole situation was out of control. The disciples had been given power to heal in the study on: "Jesus Sent Out His Disciples," Matthew 9:35-38; 10:1-42; Mark 6:6-13; and Luke 9:1-6. They had been successful on their mission. But now they had failed. Was it a lack of faith and prayer? Could it also have been their attitude? The arguing in the study was among the disciples about position, prestige, and superiority. They were failing at what Jesus had been teaching them by word and example. They had not grasped the idea of a kingdom of loving servants. The power structures of empire still controlled their thinking. No wonder Jesus was frustrated. Would they never learn?

During all that was going on the father and boy break through the crowd. The father falls at Jesus' feet and pleads, "Lord have mercy on my son, for he has seizures...." (Matthew 17:15). Some translations have "epileptic." The Greek word means "moon struck," by the evil moon goddess, Selene. The description given about the boy is very graphic and gruesome. No wonder the man asks Jesus to have pity on them and if he can, heal him. Jesus responded, "Everything is possible for him who believes." "I do believe, help me overcome my unbelief," the man replied (Mark 9:22-24). The verses that follow tell about Jesus healing him.

It is amazing how Jesus, during all the turmoil and his own frustration with the disciples, took time with the man. He healed the son and gave him to his father.

This is the last of nine studies of Jesus on retreats teaching the disciples. After all that, you would expect this study to be about graduating and diplomas handed out. Not so. It is as though Jesus is beginning again from the beginning. Read the remainder of Mark 9 and Luke 9 to see what Jesus taught them about how they were to be servants. Again, he told them that he was going to Jerusalem and there be killed. They had so much yet to learn. There are many lessons relevant both in the story of the boy being healed and, in the teaching, that Jesus gave to the disciples.

Application to Life

Faith is a trust relationship not a button to push to get what you want. Faith gives hope. It gives hope for healing, but also hope for strength, grace, and courage if there is no healing. We all shall die. Sometimes there are miraculous healings from God. Sometimes there are miraculous healings from God through medical science. Sometimes healing does not come. Faith, relating in trust to God, is important in all three scenarios or others you might know.

Prayer is also important, not just to let your desires be known, but to listen for God as he speaks through friends, the Bible, circumstances, the quiet voice of your conscience or so many other ways. Prayer is being still before God, knowing that he is with you and cares for you more than anyone.

Attitude affects life. Beware, learn from the disciple's mistakes. "I am better than…" "They or you are not as good as…." "I want first place in." You complete the list of non-Jesus like attitudes. They are dangerous. Replace them with servant ideas. Make a list of how you might change in attitude toward yourself and others.

Jesus Taught at the Feast of Tabernacles
John 7:11-52

There were three major festivals or feasts in the Jewish calendar. Passover, in the first month of the year celebrated God's deliverance of Israel from Egyptian bondage. Fifty days later, or seven weeks, was Pentecost (fifty) or the Festival of First Fruits. The third was the Festival of Booths or the end of harvest. The people lived in booths for a week. The booths were constructed of poles, limbs and brush. They remembered and celebrated how their ancestors lived in booths in the wilderness when they escaped from Egypt. You may read about these festivals in chapter twenty-three of Leviticus in The Old Testament.

The setting for this study is in Jerusalem. According to John's Gospel, Jesus made four trips to Jerusalem (John 2:3; 5:1; 7:10; 12:12. It was mid-week of the Festival of Booths. In John's story, Jesus did not come at the beginning. Was this because he might be recognized when less people were there? By the time he arrived there were crowds there.

Chapter seven of John's Gospel has several conversations of Jesus with different people. His recorded teaching is brief and to the point. He revealed the source of his teaching. He taught of the danger of judging others. He told that he would depart, but the Spirit of God would come to them.

Jesus went to the temple to teach. The crowd was there. Confusion about Jesus abounded. Imagine their questions about him. Listen, can you hear them? "Where did he get so much wisdom? " "Don't we know his family? " "Can he really be the Messiah?" "Is he not wanted by the authorities?" "Why have they not arrested him?" "Have they decided that he is the Messiah?" Messiah means the anointed one. The one awaited by Israel who would set them free from Rome. In Greek the word is Christ. Jesus is his name. Christ is a title. The Jews expected a king like David, a military ruler. Jesus did not meet that criteria, but he did meet the criteria of the prophets who talked of a day when swords will be turned in to plows and spears into pruning hooks. Nation will not lift sword against nation, they will learn war no more. Read this in Isaiah 2:4.

You may have noted that John used the word Jews to speak of Jesus enemies. The other gospels are more specific and speak of some Pharisees and **some** Sadducees being Jesus enemies. The word Jews should not stir anti-Semitic feelings. Remember, Jesus was a Jew

Jesus plainly taught them that his message was from God. This would infuriate those who did not believe him to be the Christ. John wrote sixty or more years after this event. By then there was a strong teaching that Jesus came from God, went to God and would return. John was emphasizing his own convictions about the person of Jesus and his relationship to God.

Many scholars believe that John 7:19-24, may have originally been in chapter 5. There, Jesus at another Jewish festival, healed a man who had been ill for 38 years. Read that story and you may see why scholars make that supposition. Never the less, the point for this study is that Jesus outsmarted his opponents and gave us a good lesson on being non-judgmental.

The "one work" may refer to the healing in chapter 5. The point Jesus made is that they performed the operation (work) of circumcision on the 8th day after birth, as required, even if the 8th day was on a Sabbath when no work could be done. Jesus point was, is it not much more proper to make a whole man whole on the Sabbath? John 7:24, "Do not judge by appearances, but judge with right judgment."

Application to Life

Do you have a sin list? That is, are there particular wrongs that your hold against others, while doing or failing to do worse things yourself. Paul made lists in several of his letters. Items in those lists are often used as proof texts to condemn others, but if you read the whole list, you will find there several things you do. Examine your attitudes, your speech, your emotions. Tale time to read the little letter of James in the N.T. as part of your application of this study.

Jesus Forgave the Woman Caught in Adultery
John 7:53; 8:1-59

If it was not so sad; this story could be humorous. Do you see the irony in it, even sarcasm? Jesus was great at defeating his opposition in nonviolent and non-abusive ways.

The setting for this study was a trap set by Jesus' religious opponents. They brought a lady before Jesus and the crowd. There was no attempt to make the "court" scene private. There was no regard for her embarrassment or perhaps her dress or undress. Her accusers said that she was caught in the very act of adultery. It would be a fair question to ask if she was caught in a trap also.? It is obvious that the man caught in the act with her was not there or was not being charged.

Her accusers told Jesus the Mosaic law. Did he not know it? But it was only part of the law. Read what they said. Leviticus 20:10, "If a man commits adultery with another man's wife-with the wife of his neighbor- **both** the adulterer and the adulteress must be put to death." Did you see the difference? So, if he was guilty, where was he? Did he get away? Was it because he was male? Was there a double standard?

Did they expect Jesus to agree with the death penalty? They were testing Jesus' loyalty to the law of Moses. They were in for the surprise of their lives. Jesus stooped and wrote in the sand. They continued to question him as he wrote. He stood, looked at them and said, "If any one of you is without sin, let him throw the first stone at her." Surprise!! Then he bent down again and continued writing. Wouldn't you like to know what he wrote? What do you think he may have written? Some think that he was making a list of the sins of which he knew the accusers were guilty.

Could he have written: Are you guilty of adultery? When did you last look in lust at this lady or another? What makes you better than this lady? Which of you has not coveted the possessions of your neighbor? We do not know what he wrote. But we do know that it hit home. When Jesus stood up no one is there but the lady. Jesus asked where they were. John wrote that they all left, the older ones first. Jesus told her that he did not condemn her. He told her to not do it again.

What a picture of mercy. She too, was a child of God. She had escaped the religious rulers trap and so had Jesus.

Do you think John told this story to illustrate the danger of false relationships? But relationships that can be changed and forgiven? In the remainder of the chapter Jesus declared directly and with metaphor his relationship to God. He also said anyone who had faith in him would know that relationship. In this section Jesus was dealing with a group of people who felt superior to others because of family tree. They claimed to have Abraham and Moses as ancestors and that gave them right relationship, special relationship to God.

In John 8:12-20 Jesus told them that he was the light of the world. To follow Jesus was to know life. He claimed his testimony was true. It was from God. And God was his witness. In John 8:21-30 Jesus told about his death and that he was "the son of man." That was a Messiah title also. He told them that when they saw him "lifted up" (crucified) they would know who he was. In verses 31 – 38 Jesus told them to follow him and they would know the truth, and the truth would set them free. Is the idea here that you learn to walk by walking? You learn more truth by living the truth you know? Verses 39-59 Jesus claimed that before Abraham was, "I am." There it is again. John makes his case over and over for the divinity of Jesus.

Application to Life

The story, verses 1-11, can really get to your conscience and attitude. Below is a list to begin your thinking or discussion. Hopefully you will add to the list and learn to have a deeper compassion for yourself and others. God is merciful. Are you?

Questions: Who are the people in your society most sinned against? Who does not get justice in court, religious or civil? Who are the outcasts, untouchables: women?   the poor? aids victims?

immigrants? another race or nationality? uneducated? mentally ill? physically handicapped? old people or young people? those of different sexual orientation? How can you show and tell these people that God loves them?

Jesus Healed a Blind Man
John 9:1-41

John chapter nine is one of, if not the longest of Jesus' healing stories in the Gospels. It unfolds in eight conversations. Each conversation has gems of truth and at least one relevant lesson. This study will devote a brief paragraph to each conversation.

Sin and suffering have always been issues in life and belief. The Jews had a strong belief that suffering was a direct result of personal sin or that of parents. See Ezekiel 18. That is often the case, but not always. Suffering has many causes. Bad decisions by others, society, industry, institutions, government and so many collective causes. Even then mystery remains about it. As for this study, the point is to not blame God. Too often someone says that it is God's will. Be careful about that. Persons are punished by sin, not punished for sin. Think about it. Is it possible that what Jesus said was, "Neither this man nor his parents sinned? But that the works of God may be made known, we must work while it is day?" He did not answer the why of the blindness. But gave the answer to what God could do about it.

So Jesus illustrated his answer. He made mud paste, anointed the man's eyes, and told him to go and wash in a certain pool. He did, and he received sight. Do you think it interesting that Jesus included the man's obedience and effort in the healing? Is the lesson here about participation in the healing and work of God?

The neighbors and those who had seen a blind man begging, argued could this be the man they knew or had seen. The man answered for himself, "I am the man." They asked how it was done. He told them. They asked who did it. He said a man named Jesus did it. Watch in the story for the progressive change in his knowledge of who Jesus was.

The man was taken to the Pharisees, religious leaders, for questioning. The healing was also a religious matter. It took place on the Sabbath. The Pharisees wanted to deny that Jesus was from God. Here is a picture of those who should see but are blind. And a blind man who is seeing. His answer to whom he thought of Jesus was that he was a **prophet**. In verse 11, he thought **a man** named Jesus. He was beginning to see the light.

The Pharisee questioned the man's parents. They confessed that he is their son and that he was born blind. But they deny knowing who gave him sight. They were afraid. They had heard that anyone who confessed Jesus as the Christ would be put out of the Synagogue. You may ask, "What kind of parents are these?"

But first ask, "What kind of religious leaders are these?" They use fear as a control tactic. The lesson from this conversation is very relevant. Fear is a terrible way to control and the church can be as guilty as empire in using it. Be very, very careful not to replace love with fear.

The man was questioned again. He was fearless in his witness. Jesus found the man and asked if he believed in the "Son of Man."

The man asked who he was, so he could believe. Jesus told him; the man believed and called him **Lord. See the progression in the man's answers? Jesus was a man, prophet, Lord.**

Application to Life

God heals spiritual blindness. None are beyond the reach of God's love. Think about your need for courage to speak your belief. What causes you to fear to speak your convictions? How would you introduce Jesus from your experience(s).

Jesus Sent Out 70 Disciples
Luke 10:1-24

This study is about how Jesus sent out seventy disciples into new territory? They were to preach the Good News of the Kingdom of God and heal the sick. To get the setting, begin reading at chapter nine verse fifty-one. Jesus had determined it time to go to Jerusalem. He sent seventy disciples ahead to prepare the way for his coming. Luke told the story of the mission of the seventy; the success of the mission; and the reward of service.

You may recall that in the 24th study in Part 3 of the Galilean ministry (Matthew 9:35-38; 10:1-42; Mark 6:6-13; and Luke 9:1-6) Jesus sent out twelve disciples to villages in Galilee. The seventy sent out in this study were probably to Judean communities. Seventy was a sacred number indicating completeness. Some think it was a universal number because the ancients believed there were seventy or seventy-two nations in the world (see Genesis 10).

The mission of the seventy disciples was to preach and to heal. To show and proclaim the way of the Kingdom of God. Here are four suggestions for walking the Kingdom way. You may want to add others.

The Kingdom of God way of living is one of peace. The disciples were instructed to offer peace where ever they went. This is peace as gift, as service, as love. Not peace by violence, greed and sword. The power of love offering peaceful relationships is stronger than armies crushing people by superior military power. It is true also on the personal level, as the mission of the seventy proved. Paul's letters begin with a greeting of "Peace to you."

A second way of the Kingdom walk is simplicity. Read again what Jesus told the seventy to take and not take with them. Basic needs of all should be met for the common good. The seventy are to demonstrate simple living. Saint Francis of Assisi took these directions literally for himself and his band of followers. Simple living demonstrated the value and dependence on relationships rather than power and possessions. The seventy were vulnerable and open to the generosity of the people they encountered: abide in the home that offered hospitality and eat the food offered. Gratitude is inferred. There is grace in giving and in receiving. The "pay" they received, food and shelter was balanced by the metaphorical food of the Kingdom they were sharing. Often Jesus accepted hospitality. He told Kingdom parables about banquets when everyone was invited. The disciple's walk was and is one of hospitality.

The fourth suggestion is that the Kingdom way is a way for volunteers. No one is forced. Everyone is invited. Forced religion is dangerous. Jesus invitation is to come and follow, come and eat, come and drink, come and take up the cross. To do these is to discover life in abundance.

The seventy returned overjoyed with their success. Many believed. Many decided to follow the kingdom way. Many were healed. Jesus described the victory in verse 18, "I saw Satan fall like lightning from heaven." Do you think Jesus is saying symbolically that love and the Kingdom of God have won the victory over powers of evil? He also took time to thank God that the way is open for all, not a select few.

Jesus responds to the excitement of the seventy by reminding them that their relationship was of prime importance. Their names were written in heaven. Rejoice in that, not in the power which had been given to them for the mission. The relationship of participation in the Kingdom way and work was the reward. They had heard and seen Jesus. They had walked and talked with Jesus. Jesus indicated that prophets had desired to see what they had seen and hear the things that they had heard. The reward is in the love. It is in work done well. It will be in the shared suffering of Jesus. Some of Luke's stories that follow will make the point that real life is in relationships of love, caring, serving, giving and being grateful.

Application to Life

Walk with your group (or alone) through the four suggested characteristics of the Kingdom walk. How could you apply these in your life? Search the scripture passage again to see what other characteristics you see. How do these apply to your life? Think about the idea of rewards. So many people see this idea as pay for good deeds, etc. Do you think the reward is here and now in the joy of participating and loving and serving?

Please read the scripture for the next study, Luke 10:25-37. It is one of the most famous stories in all literature. The story of the Good Samaritan is a mirror into which you must look. Look at each character in the story. Which one reminds you of yourself? Do you see a little of each character in yourself?

Jesus Told About the Good Samaritan
Luke 10:25-37

The Gospel of Luke has seventeen stories and parables not found in the other three Gospels; Matthew, Mark, & John. The story of the Good Samaritan is one of them.

To get the point of the story you must know about the Samaritans. They lived in the territory between Galilee to the north and Judea to the south. In 722 B.C. the northern kingdom of Israel was defeated by the Assyrians. The "well and able" were exiled to various places over the Assyrian empire. They became known as the "ten lost tribes." Many exiles were moved in and intermarried with those Jews left behind. This intermarriage was against Jewish law. The descendants of these marriages became known as Samaritans. Samaria became the name of the territory and main city. The Jews had no dealings with them. There was exceptional racial and religious prejudice. Stop here and read the Gospel of John chapter four about Jesus' conversation with a Samaritan woman. It will throw light on the Jewish-Samaritan prejudices.

As you read and study the conversation in this study from Luke 10, you may want to ask yourself several times during the study, "who is my Samaritan?" Or compare yourself to each of the characters in the story. Which are you most like?

The study is a conversation between Jesus and an expert in the study of Jewish law; the ten commandments and their interpretation. The lawyer asked Jesus a question. "Teacher, what must I do to inherit eternal life?" The question is of utmost importance. But we are told that he asked the question to test Jesus. Was his question sincere? You hope so. Was his motive pure? It probably was not. The Jewish religious leaders were seeking cause to arrest him. For many people "eternal life" would suggest life after death. It can be understood that way. It more likely carries the idea of the good, just, right, quality of life here and hereafter. It begins now, not after death.

Jesus asked, "What does the law say? How do you read it?" Turning the question on the questioner Jesus was saying that, "you are the expert in law, what does it say?" This method of teaching was often used by Jesus. The rabbis habitually asked questions and argued the meaning of the laws. The lawyer had an excellent answer for Jesus. "'Love the Lord your God with all your heart and with all your soul and with all your strength and with all your mind'" and "'Love your neighbor as yourself.'" These are quotes from Deuteronomy 6:5 and Leviticus 19:18, in the Old Testament. How did the lawyer come up with that answer? Is it possible he had heard Jesus say that?

Jesus said. "You have answered correctly." "Do this and you shall live." It is recorded that Jesus had given this answer on at least two occasions. Matthew 22:34-40 where a lawyer questioned him, and he quoted these verses and said that all the law and prophets hang on these two commands. The other passage is Mark 12:28-34. That is, it! Do this and live. What you have in proper relationship to God is returning his love, because he first loved you I John 4:7-12. And we show our love to God by loving others. Love means an active concern for the good of self and others. This may vary in emotion from one relationship to another. The idea is compassion, care, concern for all people and individual persons; because all are created in God's image and he loves all.

Wanting to justify himself and hoping the answer would not be what he knew or feared that it might be, he asked, "And who is my neighbor?"

Jesus told the famous story of how a robbed and beaten man was neglected by his own race and religious leaders but helped by a Samaritan. One with whom he had no dealings. Then Jesus asked the lawyer, "Which of these three do you think was a neighbor to the man who fell into the hands of robbers?"

The Lawyer: "The one who had mercy on him" (the victim). Jesus: "Go and do likewise."

Application to Life

This will require soul searching and honesty. Who are your "Persons in the ditch?" They may be so different from you. What do you do? Put yourself in the place of each person you listed. Was the person of another race, social class, nationality? What was their need? What should you do to help? Did you fail to help? How did they act and why? Remember it is the "enemy" who does the good deed to you. Has that happened to you?

Look for opportunities to be a Good Samaritan.

Jesus Healed a Mute Man
Luke 11:1-36

This and the next five studies will be on stories about Jesus from six consecutive chapters in Luke. Each study may not include the entire chapter. This is a good place to recall that the Gospels are not biographies of Jesus, at least by today's standards. Also, be reminded that these studies are simply a survey approach to the Gospels.

With that in mind, Luke chapter eleven could be divided as: Jesus taught about prayer verses 1-13; Jesus healed and taught about unclean spirits, verses 14-28; Jesus taught about signs and light, verses 29-36; Jesus taught about values for life, verses 37-53. This study will concentrate on the first three.

The "Our Father" prayer that is prayed in thousands of homes and churches every week is found in Matthew chapter 6. Luke's shorter version of the prayer is in this study. You may want to compare the two prayers. Both deal with praise for God and the desire for his will to be done. Both are prayers for daily physical needs and relationship needs such as; provisions, forgiveness, and protection.

Luke then adds two lessons about prayer. The story is of a persistent, determined, and late-night traveler who knocks until the man of the house opens and invites him to come in. It was a one room house with a family of parents and children sleeping on the floor. Everyone would be disturbed. But persistence paid off.

Many may interpret Jesus as teaching that persistent prayer to God gets results. This could be true. But closer reading may lead you to see that the main lesson is one of comparison. That is the man opened the door because of persistent knocking, but God knows you as his child. If a parent would not give a snake to his child when the child had asked for fish, HOW MUCH MORE will God give his Spirit. HOW MUCH MORE is God gracious, loving, generous, and faithful.

The "knock, seek, find" verses could be saying that you are invited to participate in your prayer answers. What do you think about that? You may pray for something you really need. Pray about it, but also work and save for it. It may be the need of another, like food or clothing. Pray for them but give to meet the need. You may pray about a decision. But use your brain to study and seek the best answer.

The man in the story was believed to be mute because of unclean spirits or demons. Jesus healed the man so that he could speak. The crowd was amazed. Jesus took the opportunity to teach a wonderful lesson; whether you believe in demons or unclean spirits. You may prefer to use psychological terms of today, such things as: bad habits, uncontrolled temper and desires, addictions, rotten attitudes etc. The lesson is: getting rid of the bad is not enough. The bad gotten rid of, left a vacancy. It must be replaced with good. Or as the story says, it will come back and bring seven worse than itself. Be good for something, not good for nothing. Paul used the idea of taking off the old and bad and putting on the new clothes. Read Paul's letter to the Ephesians 4:21-5:2 in the New Testament of your Bible.

After Jesus told the crowd that an evil generation seeks after signs, he told them they had been given a sign in Jonah. He reminded them that the people of Nineveh had repented when warned by Jonah. But a greater than Jonah, Jesus had come to them to preach God's love and Kingdom. He had healed the sick, he had showed them how to live and yet they desired to kill him instead of following him. Read the short book of Jonah in the Old Testament. It will show you how much God has always loved all people.

As to the passage about light and the eyes; the lesson has to do with willingness to hear and do God's will. As with other teachings of Jesus, bad things come from the heart because bad things are allowed in. Jesus is the light of the world. Let him into your inner being and obey him. That way you reflect his light to others. It is important what you see and read and hear. Seek the truth. All truth is from God.

Application to Life

Think about or discuss "Our Father" prayer and compare it to the one in Matthew 6. Note in Matthew the "Thy kingdom come, thy will be done on earth as in heaven." What does that say about the here and now? Rethink and discuss the participatory prayer idea. Discuss the things in your life that need casting out. What good things will you put in their place? Do you want signs or trust in God with evidence you have by experience?

Jesus Told About a Rich Fool
Luke 12:1-59

The story for this study is in verses 13-21. Chapter twelve of Luke has several characters, conversations, and two stories. If your Bible has paragraph headings there may be as many as eight sections. Do you see any common topics in these sections? Why would Luke put all these segments together? Was he stringing events and stories together as he heard them from those who had seen and heard Jesus?

For this study the assumption is that the central story is that of the rich farmer and a key verse is 21, "This is how it will be for anyone who stores up things for himself but is not rich toward God." Another key verse is 34, "For where your treasure is, there your heart will be also." These two verses are like the ends of a shoe lace. Bring them together and tie a knot that binds the lessons of the whole chapter together. The summary could be; take off your mask, trust God and be a good steward. Brief and blunt, don't be a fool. See if you think the surrounding teachings of the chapter help to give meaning to the farmer story. They help in understanding and changing three characteristics of foolishness: lack of genuineness, lack of gratitude and lack of generosity. Add it up and you have lack of grace.

The rich farmer was self-centered and a hypocrite. Jesus had warned the disciples to beware of the yeast of the Pharisees which was hypocrisy. That means thinking and acting like someone you are not. For the Pharisees it was self-righteousness or feeling superior to others. The farmer thought that he was special and had brought about the abundant crop on his own. Some estimate that 90% of crop success depends of things of nature.

His attitude, about living for years and hording the crop, says a lot about his feeling of superiority over things for which he had no control. Hypocrisy comes from Greek plays where characters wore masks. Jesus is saying that is foolish in real life. Take off your mask. Be your best self. To help with this read Romans chapter twelve in the New Testament, where the Apostle Paul wrote in verse three, "Do not think of yourself more highly than you ought...." His actions show he lacked gratitude. He tears down barns to build bigger ones. There is no sign of gratitude to God or anyone else for the large crop. About ten times in the short story the farmer used first person, personal pronouns: me, my, myself, and I. Again, in the surrounding verses Jesus made a big emphasis on trusting God to provide for your needs.

You may find it interesting that Luke used a large paragraph found in the Sermon on the Mount. Compare Luke 12:22-32 with Matthew 6:25-34. It is a dangerous position when a person thinks he or she is self-made and independent of others and God. Gratitude is a foundation stone in relationships with others and God. Grace is the root word of gratitude. Did he know, God said in Deuteronomy 8:17-18: "Do not say to yourself, 'My power and the might of my own hand have gotten me this wealth.' But remember the Lord your God, it is he who gives you power to get wealth…"

True gratitude, thanksgiving leads to generosity. The farmer's treasure and security were in barns filled with grain. The more the better. No mention of the poor. No mention of giving. Rather it said, "eat, drink, be merry." No thought of or for others. This is so relevant when in today's world ONE PERCENT OF THE WORLDS POPULATION CONTROLS HALF **OF THE WORLD'S WEALTH.** World hunger is a major problem for the poor and children while the "barns" of the rich overflow. Much of the remaining conversation and another story in chapter twelve deal with faithfulness and trust in God. The faithful stewards on the job in the master's absence. Faithfulness is having your heart in the right place. What persons do with their time, money and possessions writes their story. The farmer was not judged or condemned for being rich or having a big crop. The problem was he was not rich toward God. How could he have been rich toward God? Genuineness, Gratitude, and Generosity lived out in a faithful trust relationship to God. Or hear again the two great commandments, love God with all your being and love your neighbor as yourself. The farmer learned the hard way that death is no respecter of persons. Your life now is very important.

Application to Life

As you begin thinking about what this means to you. Remember that possessions may be one of the most difficult issues to deal with. How much is enough? When are we being generous enough? What standard of living is right? What makes the difference between a need and a want? Many organizations feed the poor, build houses, drill water wells, teach money management, job training and do healing ministry. To which should you or your church give?

Jesus Healed a Woman Who Was Bent Over
Luke 13:1-21

There have been many stories of Jesus healing persons in this long series of studies on the life and teachings of Jesus. There are more to come in the remainder of the studies. Each story is unique. The stories may differ as to disease, place, gender, faith, race, religion, requests, and circumstances. Jesus 'compassionate love and power to heal are the constants.

This story takes place in a Synagogue (a local Jewish place of worship and study) on a Sabbath day. The sick one, or victim, is a woman. Her problem is a bent back. She was so bent over she had to face the ground. In the passage for this study, Jesus healed the woman and made several statements, before and after her healing, that spoke about current circumstances and the kingdom of God.

As a good Jew, Jesus continued to attend Synagogue on the Sabbath. So, did a woman who had some form of back disease. It was so bad that she was bent over and had been in that condition for eighteen years. Do you think she might have been a regular Synagogue participant despite her condition? Did she know Jesus or who he was? If she did, why do you think she did not approach him? Why did she not ask him to heal her?

Rather, Jesus called to her to come to him. The story does not record her requesting anything. Jesus told her that she was free from the disease. He indicated that she had been bound by Satan. She stood straight when Jesus spoke, and she began praising God.

The leader of the Synagogue did not speak to her or to Jesus, but to the crowd. He said, "There are six days for work. Come and be healed on those days, but not on the Sabbath." The healing was considered work and work was not to be done on the Sabbath.

Jesus over heard what was said. He asked in his calm and confident manner, "You, hypocrites! Doesn't each of you on the Sabbath untie his ox or donkey from the stall and lead it out to give it water? Then should not this woman, a daughter of Abraham, who Satan has bound for eighteen long years, be set free on the Sabbath day from what bound her?" The leaders or opponents of Jesus were humiliated, but the people praised God for what Jesus was doing.

As with Luke chapter twelve, so with chapter thirteen, the story is surrounded by teachings about the Kingdom of God. The verses preceding the story are difficult to understand because they refer to some historical situations about which information is not complete. The verses that follow the story are some easier to understand. A few suggestions for you to consider. Could the woman with the bent back, bound by Satan, suggest that some in the religious system are bent out of shape? When did animals become more important than persons? Does this, as the other healings Jesus did, say that this is what the Kingdom of God is about: setting people free?

The metaphors mustard seed and yeast are found in Matthew's Gospel also. The Kingdom grows so large that birds (nations) come to find rest there? The yeast, working invisible in the dough, permeated the whole loaf. The Kingdom too, works that way.

Keep in mind there are at least five emphases in Luke that relate directly to the Kingdom of God. If you haven't noticed, take a quick look back and then forward at the study headings. Look for prayer, Holy Spirit, women, poor other marginalized people, and inferences that the Gospel is universal. God loves his whole creation.

Another Kingdom of God idea in this chapter is the Kingdom of God is like a banquet to which all are invited. Banquet and meal sharing will appear in other studies. There is something about breaking bread, eating together, that brings people closer together. Jesus often ate with whoever invited him and sometimes invited himself. At least he told Zacchaeus that he was going home with him Luke 19.

Application to Life

Discuss or think about how institutions and rules may become so important that the needs of persons may be overlooked. Are there customs or biases that make it difficult to help others? Can you think of people that you should have a meal with in order to befriend or help them? How do you think eating together breaks down barriers?

Why do you think the bent over woman was at the Synagogue? Did she go to find Jesus? Why do you think Jesus did what he did and said what he said? Would you have had the courage to do and speak as he did? Does the healing story relate to the teachings that follow?

Part 6
Jesus' Perean Ministry

Jesus Dined with A Pharisee and Healed A Man
Luke 14:1-25

This is the first of eight studies on Jesus' Perean ministry. Perea was an area east of the Jordan River. In this study Jesus was invited to the home of a leader of the local Synagogue who was a Pharisee. The story has the "makings" of a set up to trap Jesus. Even though his followers and admirers were increasing, so were his opponents.

Was the sick man invited to the meal? That may be doubtful, because after Jesus healed the man, he sent him away. The man was said to have dropsy. Dropsy is an old and less technical term for edema. Edema is a swelling caused by excess fluid trapped in the body's tissues. It may be caused by heart failure, kidney disease, or cirrhosis of the liver.

In this passage Jesus healed the man and taught lessons about common manners and the way of life in the Kingdom of God.

It is as though Jesus recognized the set up. He had gone to the home of a Pharisee on the Sabbath, for a meal. Present was a man with dropsy. Jesus asked the lawyers and Pharisees if it was lawful to heal on the Sabbath. They were silent. They gave no answer. So, Jesus healed the man and sent him away. Then Jesus asks them if they had a donkey or an ox to fall into a well, would they not rescue it on the Sabbath. Still, they gave no reply. Surely this aroused the suspicion of Jesus and the other guests. Why would they have remained quiet?

Jesus had noticed how the guests vied for the places of honor at the table. He gave them a lesson on manners. When invited to a banquet, do not go in and sit at the head of the table or place of honor. It would be embarrassing to you and the host to ask you to move. Rather take a lower place, and if you are to be one of the honored ones, the host will come and get you. Lesson: "Do not think of yourself more highly than you ought to think." Romans 12:3. The kingdom way is, the first last and the last first. It has servant, not a lord it over spirit.

When you give a banquet, he said to the host, don't invite those who will invite you in return. Rather, invite the poor, lame, blind and others who cannot repay you in kind. Lesson: "It is more blessed to give than to receive…" Acts 20:35. Read Matthew 25:31-45.

Do you think Jesus' word about a banquet made the guest think of God's Kingdom being like a banquet? Jesus responded to the man's "blessing" by telling a story of a banquet. What do you think of those who were invited but made excuses why they could not go? The point of the story may have been shocking to all. Everyone is welcome. Bring those least expected to be invited.

The scene switches from the banquet room to the road. Crowds are following Jesus. There must have been many reasons for their following. Jesus turns to them with a startling statement. What do you think Jesus meant by using the word hate? Was it to get attention? Was he teaching by comparison, that it is in putting love for God first, you can learn to correctly love your parents and others? The conclusion of the matter according to Luke is to be salt. Salt of the earth. Preserving, protecting, healing, flavoring all around you through love.

Application to Life

Should you and/or your group throw a party and invite the poor, lame, blind….? Who would the outcasts of your society be. Dare you befriend one? Do you think that would be Jesus like? Do you even know one of these people?

Jesus Told About the Prodigal Son
Luke 15:1-32

You may want to consider another title for this famous story by Jesus. Why not call it the story of **two prodigal sons**? Or, **an extravagant father?** Or just call it **home coming**. What title would you give it and why?

According to Bible scholars, this chapter in Luke is a part of Jesus' Perean ministry. Perea is an area east of Jerusalem and across the Jordan River. The context is another time when Jesus is being criticized by the Pharisees. You may already know that the Pharisees were Jewish religious persons who were strict about keeping the law of Moses, but also the traditions that elders had added over many years. They were accusing Jesus of associating with publicans and sinners, even eating with them; all against those traditions. Publicans were Jews who collected taxes, for Rome, from the Jews. They were sometimes considered traitors.

The three stories Jesus tells make the point that God loves his whole creation and goes to extremes to find and save it. There is a lost sheep. Is there irony in the story? What shepherd would leave 99 sheep in the wilderness to go and find one that is lost? But God does!! The woman searching for the coin may be more realistic. You can just see her turning her house (probably one room house) upside down looking for the coin till she finds it. This study is about the lost boy. But, note that all three stories end in a celebration, a party. What does that say to you about the love of God? The story of the Prodigal Son is the story of everyone. The Father shows the character of God. Either boy could be every or any person. Jesus revealed to us the character of God.

For whatever reason, the younger son asks for his inheritance, leaves home to be independent and wastes all that he has been given. He was dependent on the grace of the father even to do that. It was as though he said to his father, "I can't wait for you to die. I want mine now." Bad choice. He was off to fun time, loose living and fair-weather friends. The good news is, he came to himself. The Twelve Step folk say you must hit bottom to look up. The prodigal did just that. It was then he realized the error of his ways, he came to himself. A picture of repentance. He turned toward his father and home.

Can you picture God running? The father saw the boy coming long before he got there. He must have looked for him a long time. He ran to meet him. The boy had a repentance speech. Don't think he got to say it all. The father called for all the signs of sonship to be brought: a robe, a ring, shoes. He was lost and came home. An old hymn has a line, "back to my Father and home."

The brother stayed home, worked, obeyed, with an attitude of jealousy? He is the only one to mention prostitutes. Was its unhappiness, thinking he had missed something? The father reminded him that all that the father had was his. He seemed never to have realized what he had, plus a double portion inheritance. He refused to go to the party given in joy over the young brother's return. Do you think he was ever reconciled? Lesson: do not let sourness make you miss the party. Be reconciled to God and your "brothers."

Back to the setting, Jesus was living the part of the Father in their presence. He accepted the tax collectors and sinners. He partied with them. The whole life and teaching of Jesus is that God loves each, and all persons, in fact the world. Jesus is saying to you and to all, "Come home."

Application to Life

Picture yourself in the role of each character. How do you fit? Are we not all sometimes like the prodigal and elder brother. How can we be more like the father? Surely you know, after reading the story, God loves you.

Jesus Told About the Rich Man and Lazarus
Luke 16:1-31

Chapter sixteen of Luke may be a continuation of Jesus' teaching in chapter fifteen, which told the stories of a lost sheep, lost coin and lost boy(s). Or it appears that Luke is stringing together another batch of Jesus' "pearls" of wisdom. The knot tying the "pearls" together is the subject of possessions and their use or abuse.

This study will deal with the story in verses 19-31, called The Rich Man and Lazarus." The story has often been used by the church to threaten people with hell in the afterlife. The word translated hell in some versions of the Bible is the word Hades or place of the dead.

The story is rather about a wasted or selfish life; about life determined by one's attitude and use of possessions made possible by the grace of God. Jesus created this story as an instrument for teaching truth about life and wealth. Do not get caught up in speculation about afterlife and miss the meaning of life here and now.

The story does not tell where or how the man got his wealth. The point of this story is what he did with his riches, or better, what his riches did to him. He "dressed in purple and fine linen and lived in luxury every day." "At his gate was laid a beggar named Lazarus, covered with sores and longing to eat what fell from the rich man's table." Does this remind you of the "rich fool" in Luke 12? There the farmer had a huge crop. He tore down old storage buildings and built larger ones. He said to himself that he had food, wealth, for many years. So, he could take his ease. So, what do you see as the common problem in both stories? Isn't this success? The one with the most wins? Isn't this the goal of life to be rich? Not so according to the story Jesus told.

The ignored contrast is the problem. The beggar was placed at the door of one who could help but was ignored. What an opportunity for being of service to mankind. Just the crumbs were desired by the beggar. What do the dogs have to do with the story?

This is one of the most relevant stories in the Gospels. When, in the world at this present time, one percent of the population own and control 50 percent **of the world's wealth; there is a problem!**

Every person deserves food, shelter, clothing and health care. But there will always be countless ones like Lazarus if there are rich people like the one in this story. Jesus created a judgment scene in the story to describe what it means to miss the meaning of life in the Kingdom of God. So, are you beginning to see how important it is to live this life in community with others. To share is Christ like. Again, riches can be useful to the whole world. Read Old Testament and New Testament, Jews and Christians, greed is damning. God is for the poor. Read again Luke chapter four. Jesus said, quoting from Isaiah (Old Testament prophet), "The Spirit of the Lord is upon me, because he has anointed me to preach good news to the **poor**. He has sent me to proclaim freedom to the prisoners and recovery of sight for the blind, to release the oppressed, to proclaim the year of the Lord's favor." Read about the Good Samaritan in Luke 10; read Matthew 25:31-43; the Book of James. The Kingdom of God has to do with the here and now. See the relevance?

Application to Life

Few studies will have more application to life than this one. If you have done the previous studies recall how many of them had to do with healing and feeding. Christ came to point us to God who cares for the needs of all people.

How can you and/or your group meet the needs of the suffering and hungry near you? Check on organizations in your community that are doing ministry. Volunteer your time and resources. Learn about Christian organizations that are serving around the world in ministries of healing and food distribution. Some organizations work in providing safe water, teaching farming, job training, child care, education, and other ways for people to have the basics of life. These are ways of showing Jesus' love and call to follow.

Jesus Raised Lazarus from the Dead
John 11:1-57

Jesus, in this study was somewhere on the east side of the Jordan River from Jerusalem. The area was known as Perea. His friends Lazarus, Martha and Mary lived in Bethany near Jerusalem. They were brother and sisters. This is not the Lazarus Jesus spoke of in the last study found in Luke 16. Jesus would visit these friends on his trips to Jerusalem.

Jesus received word that Lazarus was ill. He decided to wait a couple of days before going to see him. In the meantime, he got word that Lazarus had died. He then decided to go. His disciples gave Jesus warning. He was a wanted man in Judea. Some Jewish religious leaders were really upset with Jesus and were determined to have him killed.

Jesus informed the disciples that Lazarus had died, and he was going to raise him from death. Thomas, one of his disciples, showed courage when he said the disciples should go with Jesus and face death with him. He said, "Let us also go, that we may die with him."

This study will discuss Jesus' conversation with the sisters, raising Lazarus, and the plot of the Sanhedrin to kill Jesus.

When Martha heard Jesus was coming, she hastened to meet him. "Lord, if you had been here, my brother would not have died. But I know that even now God will give you whatever you ask." Was this a word of disappointment followed by a strong statement of faith? "Your brother will rise again," Jesus said. Martha's reply, "I know that he will rise again in the resurrection at the last day." That was a wonderful statement of faith. Many Jews did not believe in resurrection. Jesus responded with one of his most quoted "I am" sayings. "I am the resurrection and the life." There, at the grave of a friend, Jesus made an awesome claim. Was he saying that life, as it was meant to be, is lived in relationship to him?

Martha went back home to tell Mary that Jesus had come, and she quietly slipped away to go to him. Mourners followed her. Mary, like Martha, said to Jesus, "Lord, if you had been here, my brother would not have died." When Jesus saw Mary and the mourners weeping, he wept. Their pain was his pain. Their sorrow was his sorrow. Death was their enemy and his. Why do you think he wept?

This event carries huge symbolic meanings. Four days in the tomb meant, no doubt he is dead. The tomb was a large cave like hole dug in the side of a rock or bank. A large rounded stone was rolled in a trench to close the opening. Jesus asked that the stone be rolled away. Then with a loud voice he called for Lazarus to come forth. He did, hands and feet bound and a cloth around his head. Jesus told them to lose him and let him go. This was awesome. Does this prefigure Jesus' resurrection? Lazarus would die again, Jesus would not. What about the unloosing and letting go? Does this story give you hope in resurrection? Do you believe that Jesus is resurrection and life for all who follow him? He gives life now and here after.

You would think that this great miracle would convince everyone that Jesus was the Christ. Not so. Though many believed, many of the religious leaders did not believe. In fact, they were more determined to have him killed. The Sanhedrin was something like the supreme court of the Jews. It was made up of seventy religious' leaders, many if not most were Sadducees. They were an aristocratic group of priests who were in control of the Temple and secured their positions by not offending the Roman rulers. Caiaphas, the high priest, had a plan. Why should they fear Jesus causing problems, if they simply turn him over to the Romans? That way they could keep their positions and their temple would be safe. Little did they know that it was not Jesus, but a rebellion about 35 years later would cause Roman soldiers to destroy the temple, never to be rebuilt. The crucifixion of Jesus was only a short time away. They seemed to have no idea that the Kingdom of God, proclaimed by Jesus, was not a military, violent rebellion. It was a WAY of life, a WAY of love and peace.

Application to Life

How did you answer the question about believing that Jesus is the resurrection? Life with meaning is found not in saying yes to a question, but giving yourself in a trust relationship to God, whom Jesus showed by word and deed to love us all.

A topic for thought and discussion from this study is FEAR. Some feared Jesus because to follow him meant giving up status, position, power, possessions. Jesus life and message are of love. John, the apostle, said perfect love casts out fear.

Jesus Healed Ten Lepers
Luke 17:11-37

This is a study about grace and gratitude. Grace was given to all; gratitude was expressed by one. The story takes place on the border between Galilee and Samaria. It will help to understand the story if you will read Leviticus chapter 13, especially verses 45-46. Also read Numbers 5:1-5. There are a variety of skin diseases called leprosy. Jesus had begun his journey to Jerusalem back in Luke 9:51. The purpose of this study is to grasp something of the importance of the grace of God and the gratitude of man. The emphasis is on the importance of expressing gratitude and how it can become a part of life and character. Jesus healed 10 lepers; one of them gave thanks; that one, a Samaritan.

Leprosy did vary degrees of serious damage to the skin and body. But the physical was only part of the suffering. Did you note in the Old Testament law how one was isolated (outside) the camp? They could not come near persons. At a distance they were to cry out a warning so that no one would come near them. They were banned from worship. There was physical, mental, emotional and spiritual suffering.

In this story the ten lepers cried out to Jesus from a distance, "Jesus, Master, have pity on us!" Jesus did have pity on them. He told them to go and show themselves to the priests. And as they went, they were healed. What a picture of grace. Refer again to Leviticus. The priest had the authority to pronounce clean and unclean. He was the diagnostician. Remember Jesus was a Jew, he respected Moses' law.

Consider for a moment this question. Why were there ten in a group? Do you suppose the group consisted of different ages, genders, vocations, nationality, races, economic and social status? Why not? Suffering tends to break down barriers and bring people together. When were you last in a hospital ICU waiting room? All kinds of people talk with each other, feel for each other, pray for each other. When were you in or heard about a natural disaster like a tornado, flood, or fire. People get together to share, grieve and express gratitude. We are not told about what this group did, but we are told what one did. One returned to give gratitude for the grace.

Do you think the one who returned went to the priest first and then came to thank Jesus? He came praising God in a loud voice, he fell at Jesus' feet and thanked him. How do you think Jesus felt? Does not everyone like to feel appreciated? Jesus asked, were there not ten? Where are the other nine? Would you have been the one or one of the nine? Should not gratitude be an automatic response to grace?

Jesus refers to the Samaritan as a foreigner. Be reminded that the Samaritans were descendants of Jews who had married foreigners and was opposed by Jewish law. The Jews and Samaritans had a wall of hate and prejudice between them. Were the other nine Jews? Does the story infer that? You only must read the Psalms to see how thanksgiving and praise of God is a foundation to Jewish religion. But somehow nine seemed to have forgotten.

Application to Life

"Little things mean a lot," so goes a line in a song. How true that is. Gratitude is so easily done and so easily neglected. To develop a habit, you must practice. So, the application of this lesson is to begin, right now, to practice the grace of gratitude. Just say, Thank you. Say it. Was that not easy? Now take some time to list for what and to whom you are thankful. Have you told them? Saying or thinking, "Thank you, Jesus" ought to be at the head of the list. Is saying and showing thanks to others a way of saying thanks to God. Is it not through others, friends and family that you are often blessed? Don't just make this about now but think back to teachers and others who helped you along the way. Make a call, send a note, go to see, send a gift. Let someone know your gratitude to them. Do it today. Thank Jesus for loving you through them.

Met with the Rich Young Ruler
Matthew 19:16-30; Mark 10:17-31; Luke 18:18-30

All three synoptic (to see with or alike) gospels tell the story of "The Rich Young Ruler." Matthew simply said "someone;" Mark called him "a man," and Luke said, "a certain ruler." The story tells that he was young and rich. It also said Jesus loved him. Keep all this in mind as you read, think about, and discuss this study. He came to the right person, Jesus. He had a very relevant question. "What must I do to inherit eternal life?" He was rich but for some reason he felt incomplete. There must be more to life than what he had. Do you think he was asking how to get to heaven when he died? Or was he seeking meaningful life here and now? Maybe both? In this study: Jesus answered his question. The man wants more; Jesus drives home the point.

"Good teacher, what must I do…." Was the man expecting Jesus to return the compliment, "Good ruler?" Hear what Jesus said. There is but one good. That is God. How do you read that? Was Jesus pointing away from himself to God? Was he answering the question with one word, God? Then he would explain how to walk in right relationship with God. Are you surprised that Jesus told him to keep the Mosaic law, the ten commandments? See Exodus 20 to read the commandments Jesus quoted to the man.

Note that the commandments Jesus quoted are those which have to do with how you treat other people: honor your parents, respect life (don't kill), respect marriage (no adultery), respect property rights (don't steal), don't even envy. The man said he did all these. Did he? Read in Matthew 5:17-48 how Jesus interprets these commandments. Don't kill, don't even hate. Don't commit adultery, don't even lust. That does tighten things up doesn't it?

You may think of the commandments as a burden, restrictions, demands. What if you see them as grace, as a gift, that to obey is to know life with meaning. Life lived without greed, envy, jealousy, hate. Life is enriched when these are replaced with love, forgiveness and gratitude. The commandments were given to a people who were being delivered from the power of Egypt. God was graciously giving them commands for a way of life in a new land of freedom. They said this is how you relate to God and how you relate to each other so that life will be good.

He felt he had kept those commands, so he asked if there was more. Jesus told him to go, sell all that he had, give it to the poor, and come follow him. Boom!! WOW! The commandments named related to person to person. But the first four commandments not mentioned deal with relating to God. Jesus put all four in that one reply. It was a quick revelation. He was trying to have more than one God. The first commandment is to have one God, only one. The second, don't make graven images. Had this man's money or houses or life style become his god? For religious people it can be a title, a temple, a Bible, a creed. What is placed before God. Third commandment don't take God's name in vain. Live your faith. Let your life reflect God's way. Fourth, remember the Sabbath. Take time to remember where you came from, and who and whose you are.

Go back to Matthew 6:19-33 to see the man's problem. What is your problem? Verse 21: "For where your treasure is, there your heart will be also." Verse 24, "No one can serve two masters. Either he will hate the one and love the other, or he will be devoted to the one and despise the other. You cannot serve both God and Money." Verse 33, But seek first his kingdom and his righteousness, and all these things will be given to you.

The man walked away, grieved because he had great riches. Life is made of choices. This man appeared to love his wealth more than God. Jesus indicated that it is very difficult for a rich man to enter the Kingdom of God. The meaning is that it is difficult for a rich man to give control (kingdom, reign) of life to God. But he is very clear that all things are possible with and for God. Do you think the question to be answered in the lesson is: who or what is in control of your life?

Application to Life

Was the problem being rich or being controlled by the riches? Make a list of what people turn into idols or false gods. Money in any society can create great problems. Is money the problem or the attitude about money? There will always be people who have more than others. Can rich and poor have greed? Make a list of probable attitudes people have toward money. Which are good and which bad?

Take some time to discuss the commandments, especially how Jesus interpreted them in Matthew 5:17-48. This goes back to the importance of relationship to God and others.

Jesus Healed Bartimaeus and His Companion
Matthew 20:17-34; Mark 10:32-52; Luke 18:31-43

In this study and the one to follow Jesus is in Jericho. There are several differences in the story for this study as told by Matthew, Mark and Luke. Matthew wrote that there were two blind beggars, the other two writers told of one. Mark said the man was named Bartimaeus. Bar means son, so son of Timaeus. Mark and Matthew said the story took place as Jesus was leaving Jericho. Luke said it took place as he entered Jericho. These are minor, but interesting details. What if there were two sight healings? One as Jesus entered the city and another as he left. This is speculation, but when you interpret the meaning of this event(s) you may decide that there were two or three sight giving miracles.

Think about this. Jericho is only a few miles from Jerusalem. Jesus knew that his "hour" was getting near. The "hour" or "time," he referred to in other places, is the time of his arrest, trial, crucifixion, burial and resurrection. Very few, if any, understood this, even though he on at least three occasions told the disciples what lay ahead for him.

Now, the healings, though they literally occurred, are metaphors of spiritual sight and blindness. Those with eyes cannot see and the blind do see. If that is the case, look how powerful these events are. Jesus healed a blind man upon entering Jericho. He heals a blind man upon leaving Jericho. And while in Jericho a publican, tax collector, named Zacchaeus, (Luke 19, the next study in this series) became a believer. All the while, no one seems to grasp that he is a nonviolent Christ. He walked a way of peace into the face of death. And through death he is raised proclaiming his victory over violence, sin, death and evil. So, this study is about restoring sight and a new walk.

According to the story, the blind man learned that Jesus was going to pass near his begging station. So, he began to cry out, "Jesus, Son of David, have mercy on me!" Some in the parade of followers tried to shush him. But the more they told him to be quiet, the louder he screamed. He got Jesus' attention. Jesus asked that the man be brought to him. Jesus asked what he wanted from him. He was not begging for coins now. "Rabbi, I want to see," the blind man said. One of the writers said Jesus touched his eyes, another wrote that Jesus told him to "Go, your faith has healed you." The man received his sight immediately.

The man called him Son of David. That was a messianic term. It was a way to describe the expected Messiah or Christ. This term had different meanings to different Jews. Son of David was the one expected to be a King like David. A warrior king who conquered enemies by violence. He, in the time of Jesus would expect the Christ to raise an army and overthrow Roman rule. As stated above, Jesus did not fit that description. Whatever the blind man meant, Jesus healed his physical sight. Do you think the man got a different opinion about Jesus as the Christ?

Do you find it interesting that Jesus told the man to "go," and the man "followed Jesus along the road?" Another translation reads "on the way." Luke added that he followed, "glorifying God." Luke also noted that "all the people, when they saw it, praised God"

Following also has two meanings here. Yes, he literally, with new sight, walked following Jesus on the road. But there is metaphor here. He was no longer a blind beggar but was following the king. He was doing the king's bidding. And others followed because of what they had seen happen to the blind man. "The way" will become a major descriptive term for what today is called Christian. The earlier followers of Jesus were said to be people of "the Way." In fact, the word Christian appears only once or a very few times in the New Testament.

The next stop on that "road" or "way" would be Jerusalem. The next study, as noted earlier, is the Zacchaeus story in Jericho. But following that, there will be several studies about how Jesus entered Jerusalem and what took place there.

Application to Life

Following is a key concept in this story. This is the heart of what it means to be a Christian. It is the decision to follow in the way of

Jesus. That is what his life and teachings are about. You might benefit by making a list of changes this requires if you seriously follow him. Such a list would include changes in thought, attitude, feelings, habits, speech, how you treat those in your home. This could take some time and might work better in a group; often honest friends can help us to see the changes we need to make and can help us make the changes. Read Romans chapter twelve in the New Testament to help you with this. And, of course, the words of Jesus in the Sermon of the Mount found in Matthew chapters five – seven. Do not get discouraged. No follower does it perfectly. Take the new life a step at a time, moment by moment. Remember you have the Spirit of God within to teach and to guide you. Do not get discouraged, it is a life time process.

Jesus Goes Home with Zacchaeus
Luke 19:1-28

Zacchaeus was a wee little man,
And a wee little man was he.
He climbed up in a sycamore tree
For Jesus he wanted to see.
And as the Savior past that way,
He looked up in the tree.
And he said, Zacchaeus, you come down
For I'm going to your house today.
For I'm going to your house today.

This little song has been taught to thousands of children over the years. The story of Zacchaeus, climbing a tree to see Jesus, is a fun and entertaining story for children. But this is an adult story with very serious life applications. The story is in some ways humorous and easy to visualize. Can you see a short little man coming to a parade? Maybe he was a little late. Crowds already lined the side of the road. He was too short to see over the ones next to the road. He found it difficult to elbow his way through. Some may have recognized him as the tax collector and were not about to let him through. So, he ran on till he found a tree he could climb. Up he went and found a good place to perch. All this, because Jesus was coming down the road. In fact, the parade was the crowd following Jesus. Sort of funny, don't you think. A public official, short, but rich, climbed a tree to see Jesus. But this was serious. Note two ideas in this study: Jesus confronts Zacchaeus and Zacchaeus showed signs of conversion or transformation. That is, Zacchaeus had a life changing experience when he met Jesus.

Do you think the crowd was surprised when Jesus stopped under the tree where Zacchaeus was waiting and watching? What about Zacchaeus? You know he must have been surprised. He got more than a good view from the tree. He got a polite order from Jesus. "Zacchaeus, come down immediately, I must stay at your house today." Zacchaeus happily did as he was told.

But, some in the crowd were displeased. "He has gone to be the guest of a sinner," they said. You see, some, maybe many of the people knew who Zacchaeus was and that he was a tax collector. Tax collectors were not held in high esteem. In fact, many felt they were traitors to their own Jewish people. Tax collectors made bids to the Roman government to collect taxes for Rome from their own Jewish people. Some were known to take advantage of the people by overcharging and pocketing the extra. Some became rich that way. Does this kind of practice sound familiar where you live? Government officials are often in office to line their own pockets at the expense of the poor.

We have no record of all that was said by Jesus or his host. We do know that Zacchaeus had a life turn around. Listen to his words, "Look, Lord! Here and now I give half of my possessions to the poor, and if I have cheated anybody out of anything, I will pay him back four times the amount."

Stop now and check out what the Jewish law required for restoration for deceiving, robbing and fraud. Leviticus 6:1-5 and Numbers 5:5-7 say that one confessing to such acts must make restitution in full and add one-fifth. Zacchaeus was willing to restore four-fold and give half of all he had to the poor. Generosity abounds when Jesus is given charge of life.

Jesus said, "Today salvation has come to this house, because, this man too, is a son of Abraham. For the Son of Man came to seek and save what was lost." Sometimes the word lost is used as a synonym of judgment or "going to hell." Lost carries the idea of going in the wrong direction. It means losing one's way. Jesus came to direct people back to God who created them. He came to teach and show how "found" life is to be lived.

Application to Life

Do you think Jesus loves those whom you consider to be gross sinners? Who are the people you know that you think of as "sinners?" Would Jesus go home with them? Would you? Do you pray for them? Is there someone to whom you owe an apology or restitution?

How may you show kindness to those who do not act like you expect?

Volunteer or give to an organization that helps the poor.

Part 7

Jesus' Final Ministry In Jerusalem

Jesus' Triumphal Entry into Jerusalem
Matthew 21:1-17; Mark 11:1-11;
Luke 19:29-44; John 11:55-57; 12:1-19

This series of studies begins what the church calls Holy Week. The week follows the things Jesus did from his entry into Jerusalem on the first day of Passover week until his resurrection on the following Sunday. This series goes through the Lord's supper Thursday evening. Begin your Bible reading with John 11:55 – 12:19. It has several things you will see that set the stage for the other passages.

Passover was a most important Celebration. It celebrated the setting free of the Jewish people from Egypt by God.

With that background in mind, the following interpretation of what happened is partially credited to New Testament scholars John Crossan and the late Marcus Borg in their book, The Last Week.

Stop here and read Matthew 21:1-17; Mark 11:1-11 and Luke 19:29-44. Then imagine two processions. One was led by Pontius Pilate and the other led by Jesus.

Whether at the same time or not the fact that Pilate had come to Jerusalem from his headquarters at Caesarea by the sea is very important. He is the man with power to crucify. Pontius Pilate was appointed by Titus, the emperor of Rome, to be Governor of Judea. He would come to the Passover, and other times of huge crowds in Jerusalem, to keep the peace. The peace he kept was by threat of sword, prison and crucifixion. So, imagine him riding on a spirited stallion, decked out in uniform, sword, and shield. There would be a host of soldiers marching and riding on horses following him. Perhaps you have seen in person or on television a military parade. So, Pilate represented an empire ruled by violence. Crowds would gather to watch, knowing the power of the emperor and his army. The Jewish people had experienced that violent and destructive power and would do so again. The Roman emperor was known by such titles as Son of God, Savior, and liberator. Do those titles sound like ones you have heard ascribed to Jesus, the Christ?

Pontius Pilate, representing the powerful, rich and violent empire, enters Jerusalem on the west. He will stay in his Jerusalem home built by Herod; as was his sea side headquarters.

Down the Mount of Olives, Jesus, his disciples and peasant followers from Galilee came into the east gate of the city. They were shouting, "Hosanna!" What do you think they were expecting Jesus to do? The donkey contrasts to the military stallion. For a prophetic word read this passage from Zechariah 9:9-10:

"Rejoice greatly, O Daughter of Zion! (Jews)
Shout, Daughter of Jerusalem!
See, your king comes to you,
 righteous and having salvation.,
gentile and riding on a donkey,
on a colt, the foal of a donkey.
I will take away the chariots from Ephraim
and the war horses from Jerusalem,
and the battle bow will be broken.
He will proclaim peace to the nations.
His rule will extend from sea to sea
and from the River to the ends of the earth."

The prophetic Christ, Jesus, is carrying out a well-planned dramatic demonstration. He is demonstrating and describing the heart of God. Here is the way he was saying in drama what he had walked and taught. God's way is not sword, power, riches and violence. His way is the way of nonviolence and love.

Read the end of Luke's account, 19:38-40: "Blessed is the king who comes in the name of the Lord! Peace in heaven and glory in the highest." Some of the Pharisees in the crowd said to Jesus, 'Teacher, rebuke your disciples.' I tell you", he replied, "if they keep quiet, the stones will cry out." The following verses tell of Jesus looking over the city and weeping. What a picture of love and compassion. Do you see the contrast?

Application to Life

Use your imagination. Spend time visualizing the two processions. Peace by power bought by sword, war and violence. Peace that comes through nonviolent love. Which way will you live? To visualize this as present day, look at your own country and powerful religious radicals. Does your government budget 50% on military compared to all other expenses? Yet the money has printed on it, "In God We Trust." Do you feel that you are controlled by fear and threat?

When empires, governments and corporations disregard the needs of the poor and needy, they are acting like Rome. The Kingdom of God is living in love, compassion and nonviolence. How will you live? Who will you follow?

Jesus Cleansed the Temple a Second Time
Matthew 21:12-13; Mark 11:12-18; Luke 19:45-48

As you begin this study you will note that the scripture is from three of the Gospels. John put this story or one like it in chapter 2 of his Gospel, at the beginning of Jesus ministry. Did Jesus "cleanse" the Temple twice? Or did John put the story there to show where and why Jesus would be brought before the Roman governor to be accused and killed?

Be reminded that this week in Jesus ministry is called Holy Week by the church. Also, take your Bible in hand and see how much of each Gospel is given to this week. (Matthew, chapters 21-28; Mark 11-16; Luke 19:28 –chapter 24; John 12:12 –chapter 20) Did you find about one third or more of the pages in each Gospel are given to that week? Must be important, don't you think? It seems the event of this study took place on Monday.

Keep in mind as you read and study the "cleansing" of the temple that Jesus was putting the Kingdom of God against two powers in his society: the hierarchy of the temple and the injustice of the Roman empire. He was a Jew by race, religion and residence. He is not attacking the Jewish religion, but the abuse of it. In this study look for what Jesus did and said. And consider why he may have done and said those things.

The temple had been the center of Jewish worship for centuries. The first temple was built by King Solomon, son of Kind David. You may want to read about the building and dedication in I Kings chapters 6 & 8. It was the place of worship and sacrifice. And though the people knew that God was everywhere, the temple was where they believed God met them. The temple had replaced the Tabernacle that Moses had used for the same purpose. Read about it in Exodus 26. In 586 B.C. the temple was destroyed by the Babylonians when the Jews of the Southern Kingdom of Israel were taken captive. By 532 B.C. some of those captives and their children could return to Jerusalem to rebuild the temple. It was a long way from being the luxurious building of Solomon. This temple would be destroyed in 70 A.D.

The priests cared for the temple. Once their position meant that they were of the Jewish tribe of Levi. By Jesus time priests were almost pawns of the Roman government. It became a political appointment, given to the well to do. From the Roman view, it was away to let the Jews worship in their way but were controlled by priests who were controlled by Rome. Any of this sound familiar? Beware of religion that tries to control the state or a state that controls religion.

What Jesus did is well described. Stop now and read what he did. The usual interpretation is that the animal sellers and money changers (both necessary) were cheating: over charging for the sacrificial animals and for changing Roman coins for temple coins. But hear his words from Isaiah 56:7, "my house shall be called a house of prayer for all nations." But they had made it a den for thieves. A den, for thieves, is a place they go to hide. So maybe, not only is there cheating in the court of the Gentiles, but the priests themselves who are in cahoots with the Romans are hypocrites. Think about it. Who's it that wants to kill Jesus? We have moved from what Jesus did and said to why.

Was Jesus preparing his followers through a dramatic action? Was he predicting the destruction of the temple building? It was destroyed by the Romans in 70 A. D. not to be rebuilt. You have heard of the wailing wall? That is all that is left of the temple.

Was Jesus foreseeing the day when his followers would come to a greater realization that they individually and collectively were the temple, dwelling place, of God. "Don't you know that you yourselves are God's temple and that God's Spirit lives in you?" (I Corinthians 3:16). Ephesians 2:19-22 says you are being built into a dwelling for God, his temple. Was Jesus saying by his actions and words that he is the temple of God? It is in him we meet God. See the Revelation 21:22, "I did not see a temple in the city, because the Lord God Almighty and the Lamb are its temple." Here John visualizes heaven as a city where the God and the Lamb (Christ Jesus) are the temple. Read in John 4:21-24 about worship.

Application to Life

First, do not be critical of Jewish worship, the temple or Jews!!Now, began to ask yourself about where you meet God. Do you see in Jesus' life and teachings what God is like, LOVE? Compassion and the golden rule are the heart of all the major religions.

Think about: do people today make church buildings more important than the worship of God? Is more money spent on church buildings than feeding the poor and healing the sick? Where do you feel closest to God?

Some Greeks Want to See Jesus
John 12:20-50

In The Gospel of John this study follows Jesus' entry into Jerusalem. That was number one in this series. If you missed that study, you may read about it in Matthew 21:1-17; Mark 11:1-11; Luke 19:29-44 and John 11:55-12:19. While reading these, go ahead and read John 12:20-50. You will see where the study gets its title. Some Greeks were in Jerusalem for the festival of Passover. This worship, celebration was in memory of and gratitude for God delivering the Jews from slavery in Egypt. Read about it in Exodus chapter 12.

Following the Greeks seeking Jesus, there are several teaching sections by Jesus. You may ask if Jesus is talking to the Greeks and his disciples or a larger crowd. It might be that John saw this as a good place to put the teachings. John was the last of the four gospels written. John would have been an old man, writing about seventy years after the events he is recording.

For this study consider: Greeks wanted to see Jesus. And Jesus taught about his mission. He told what was required to follow him.

There were Greeks who had come to the Passover festival. We are not told if they were Jewish proselytes. Were they truth seekers, philosophers, or just curious? What do you think? To get an idea of the Greeks of Athens in the first century, read Acts 17:15-34. Verse 21, "All the Athenians and the foreigners who lived there spent their time doing nothing but talking about and listening to the latest idea."

Whoever these Greeks were and why they wanted to see Jesus, they came to the right person, Philip. Philip was from Galilee. Did they know that? Jesus was from Galilee. That makes it a good reason to ask Philip. Guess what, Philip takes them to Andrew. Recalling John 1 Philip had told Nathanael about Jesus. Nathanael had responded with a question, "Can anything good come out of Nazareth?" Nazareth was Jesus' home town. Maybe Philip felt more comfortable having Andrew 's presence in taking the Greeks to Jesus. Andrew was Simon Peter's brother. Growing up with quick tempered Simon would have equipped Andrew for dealing with conflict if these

Greeks became rude. Do you find it more comfortable in facing strangers if you have a trusted friend with you?

It is at this point in the study that Jesus talks with them. He uses the word glorified to describe what is shortly to take place. It was another way of saying what he had already told them at least three times. The glory would come through his self-giving death and rising from the dead. He speaks of it as destroying the power of evil.

He said that when he was lifted (crucified) he would draw all men (persons) to himself. One translation reads "all things." Verse 32, "But I, when I am lifted up from the earth, will draw all men unto myself." Wonderful! Add verse 47b, "I did not come to judge the world, but to save it." He does say that his word would judge. Could he mean the commandments? What were they? He summed it up, "love God with all your heart, soul, mind and strength. And love your neighbor as yourself." See Matthew 22:34-40.

Pick up here from the paragraph above. What is Jesus command for his followers? John 13:34-35, "A new command I give you. Love one another. As I have loved you, so you must love one another. By this all men will know you are my disciples, if you love one another." You love God by loving others.

A second word Jesus uses in this study is the word servant. If you are to be his disciple, you are to serve him. How do you serve him? You love Jesus by serving others. Read some acts of service in Matthew 25:31-46:visit the sick, care for widows and fatherless, visit the prisoners, feed the hungry, clothe the naked. Add to this list. The idea is to do unto others like you would have then do to you, see Matthew 7:12. Action is required, not just beliefs and words. By your service and love people will recognize you as a disciple of Jesus.

A third word used by Jesus in this study is light. He says he is the light and we should walk in that light. Could this carry ethical overtones? Walking in the light is living justly and acting with mercy toward others. Such words as integrity and honesty may come to mind.

Application to Life

You might think about and discuss building relationships based on this study. Make a list of questions like: do I know anyone who is a "Greek?" That is someone of another race, religion, ethnic background. What about your relationship to those who may be looked down on in your society because of a disease, sexual orientation, or social class, think of ways you can befriend these people. Keep in mind that to love and serve them, is to love and serve Jesus.

The Rulers Tried to Trap Jesus
Matthew 21:23-46; 22:1-46; Mark 11:27-33; 12:1-10; Luke 20:1-47

Jesus was at the temple, probably in the large area known as the Court of the Gentiles. What took place could remind you of a press conference. There was a crowd listening to Jesus, but several the temple rulers were near the front and began asking questions. Do you think they raised their hands to be the next to ask a question?

Before the questions are addressed in this study, there are several things to remember. Jesus was a Jew by race, religion and residence. Jesus is not opposed to the Mosaic law of God. His opponents belong to the temple leadership. They have clout with the Roman government officials. They were wealthy or would not have their positions and power. They were jealous of Jesus' popularity with the crowd and they feared anything that would threaten their power, positions. or prestige.

Now look at the questions. There are several and only a few suggestions will be made about each question. Each deserves your deeper study.

The first question relates to Jesus speaking with authority. Their teachers would quote what had been said by other rabbis. Take time now to read Matthew 21:23-27; Mark 11:27-33; and Luke 20:1-8. The question probably referred to what he said and did at the temple on the day before. He had driven out the money changers and had said that the temple had become a den for robbers but should be a house of prayer for all nations.

This was a trap. If Jesus says his authority comes from God or himself, they will accuse him of blasphemy. If he says his authority is from man, the crowd will leave. They believe he is speaking God's word. So, Jesus turns the table on them by asking where John the Baptist got his authority. If they answer his question, he will answer their question. He put them in a dilemma. If they say John's message was from God; it was John who commended Jesus as the one from

God. If they say from man, they feared the crowd, because the crowd believed John. They refused to answer.

Now, read Matthew 21:33-46; Mark 12:1-12; and Luke 20:9-19. To help with understanding Jesus' story, read Isaiah 5:1-7. The opponents of Jesus recognize themselves as the tenants in Jesus' story. They are the ones guilty of leading the people of Israel astray. Be careful not to confuse all Israel with a group of religious leaders who misled the people.

Read Matthew 22:15-22; Mark 12:13-17; and Luke 20:20-26. This was another trap. The question was whether to pay Roman tax or not. If Jesus said yes, they accuse him of being a traitor to Israel. If he said no, they use it to accuse him to Rome as a traitor to Rome. The wisdom of Jesus continued. The coin Jesus called for had the emperor's image. Jesus said give to Rome what belongs to Rome and to God what belongs to God. What does that say to you? What belongs to Rome? Does not everything belong to God? Was he saying under Roman rule taxes were required, but ultimate loyalty belongs to God? You may have to return a tax to keep peace, but real peace is found in obedience to God? The trap setters do not know how to answer. They did not get what they needed to bring Jesus to Roman court.

Read Matthew 22:23-33; Mark 12:18-27; and Luke 20:27-40. This question was based on Old Testament law called Levirate Marriage. Read about it in Deuteronomy 25:5-10. A man marries his brother's childless widow in order to have an heir for his brother. See how a similar event happens in the beautiful story in the book of Ruth. The question proposed by Jesus' opponents; it is almost ridiculous. Again, Jesus' wisdom may have raised more questions than answers. Will there be no gender or marriage in the afterlife? What does it mean to be like the angels? The major point Jesus may have made was that God is the God of the living and then names Abraham and others long since gone; but still live. Remember Jesus was under attack. And, you don't have to know all the answers. There is tremendous mystery about God. No one knows all. Beware of anyone who thinks or acts as if they do.

Read Matthew 22:34-39 and Mark 12:28-34. Are you not glad this question was asked? It may have been asked as a trap. But Jesus gave the answer to life. How to have life. Love God with all your being and love your neighbor as yourself. You may remember that Luke 10 has these two commandments. The first law is found in Deuteronomy 6:5 and the second in Leviticus 19:18.

Application to Life

Give some serious thought to each of these passages but remember there are many interpretations to some of them You don't have to know everything. Following Jesus is a matter of faith. Spend more time on thinking and discussing how you can obey the two great commandments. Memorize them. How can you show love to others? This may be a good time to discuss again the relationship of church and state.

Jesus Taught His Disciples on the Mount of Olives
Matthew 24:1-51; 25:1-46; Mark 13:1-37; Luke 21:1-38

Mark is believed to be the first Gospel written. Matthew and Luke contain a large portion of Mark's material. They made additions and deletions. It would be good before you read this study to read all the lengthy passages above. Why not read Mark first, then watch where Matthew and Luke differ from Mark and each other?

Jesus and his disciples were leaving the temple. The disciples look back and comment on the magnificence and beauty of the temple. To their surprise Jesus makes a prophetic statement that the time is coming when one stone of the temple will not sit upon another. Can you imagine how they must have felt? The temple was the center of Jewish worship. Solomon had built the first temple about 900 years earlier. It replaced the tabernacle or tent used as a symbol of God's presence and place of worship when the Jews escaped Egypt with Moses. Solomon's temple had been destroyed by the Babylonians in 586 B.C.E. present temple was originally built about fifty years later by Jews returning from Babylonian/Persian captivity. That temple was redone and vastly expanded by Herod.

The Jews of the Old Testament knew that God was everywhere. An example: "Where can I go from your Spirit?

Where can I flee from your presence?
If I go up to the heavens, you are there.
If I make my bed in the depths, you are there.
If I rise on the wings of the dawn,
If I settle on the far side of the sea,
even there your hand will guide me,
your right hand will hold me fast." Psalm 139:7-10

Why not stop and read the entire Psalm now? Also read Solomon's prayer in the temple he built in I Kings 8:27. For the Jews, the temple was a special place of worship. You can do further study of the temple with a Bible Dictionary.

No wonder the disciples were shocked. The prediction of Jesus about the temple's destruction came true between 66 and 70 A.D. The Jews rebelled again against Rome and during those years the Roman's mercilessly destroyed Jerusalem and the temple.

Much of what Jesus had to say would call to memory of the disciples the desecration of the temple by Antiochus in 164 B.C. The Romans had destroyed the Temple by the time Matthew and Luke were written, maybe, even before Mark was written.

For many, these passages are taken to be about the return of Christ, end times, or the consummation of the kingdom of God. Careful study requires that the destruction of Jerusalem and temple signs not be confused with signs of end time. That isn't easy. Note one sentence which says all this will take place before this present generation passes. If that refers to the "second coming," was Jesus wrong in his prediction? Many have been led astray and lead others astray by making these passages fodder for end time predictions. So be very careful not to get carried away by false teachers who say they know when Jesus will return because Jesus said no one knows, not even himself. Those predictions are made every generation. It seems to be an ego thing. "Since I am here Jesus will come."

What Jesus did in these passages is give hope and encouragement to his disciples and to all who trust him. God's kingdom will be consummated. God will win. Jesus died for the whole world. God loves the whole world. You do not have to know the how, when and where. It is enough to know that God is love. Jesus calls his followers to be loyal. He told them and us to watch, pray, and work. Live as if he may come today. Serve as though needs must be met by you for generations to come.

Jesus warned that as he would be persecuted, so would his followers. Later, you may study The Book of Acts. It tells how these disciples continued the teaching, preaching and healing ministry of Jesus and were persecuted. Some became martyrs.

Application to Life

As you do your study, do not get caught up in the violence and gore. Consider that God is love. Jesus and his followers were nonviolent. The later Old Testament prophets gave advise very similar to the teachings of Jesus. Read some of these passages to get an idea of God's work and expectations of his people: Micah 6:8 "He has showed you, O man, what is good. And what does the Lord require of you? To act justly and to love mercy and to walk humbly with your God." Isaiah 2:4 "He will judge between nations and will settle disputes for many peoples. They will beat their swords into plowshares and their spears into pruning hooks. Nation will not take up sword against nation, nor will they learn war anymore."

Think about and discuss peacemaking, nonviolence, and participating in living that way. What would you do if you knew this was your last day in this life? How should you live to be ready for the coming of the Lord? Think about it, he is here now.

Jerusalem Jesus Ate with Simon the Leper
Matthew 26:6-13; Mark 14:3-9; John 12:2-8

In previous studies it was noted that many Jesus' teachings occur at meals. You could call it table talk. He would eat with friend and foe. He ate with strict law keepers like the Pharisees and with known "sinners." In this study Jesus is eating at the home of one called Simon the leper. You think this was a man whom Jesus had healed? Could he have had the disease so long that he was called Simon the leper even after he was healed?

John, writing about 30 years after Mark and Matthew said the meal was at Lazarus 'home, whom Jesus raised from the dead. Lazarus' sister Martha served. Maybe this was a joint hosting. Which house and who was host are not the main concerns. What happened is very important.

There was a woman present besides Martha. John said it was Mary. Martha had a sister named Mary. Jesus visited in their home when in the Jerusalem area. Mary had a very expensive jar of perfume. As you read it was worth 300 days common labor pay. During the meal Mary opens or breaks the jar and anoints Jesus head. (Mark 14:3) and feet (John12:3). She wipes his feet with her hair. Luke 7:36-50 has a similar story. Fragrance filled the room. Those present knew it to be expensive. Criticism began. John blamed Judas for being critical. In fact, John wrote that Judas was a thief.

Here are three suggestions to consider as you study what happened. The woman, Mary believed that Jesus was going to die. Her critics were greedy, not benevolent.

An emphasis of Mark's Gospel is that very few recognized Jesus as the son of God, a nonviolent Messiah. According to Matthew's Gospel, Jesus had told the disciples at least four times that he was going to Jerusalem, would be arrested and killed. They could not get their minds around this. This woman did. She was anointing him for burial. If he was going to die, this may be the only opportunity Mary would have to show her love, an extravagant love.

Do you suppose the fragrance stayed with Jesus the remainder of the week? If so, it would remind him that there was one who believed and showed it in an act of love. She loved him even if his nonviolence led him to death

Can you hear the whispering? And someone said it out loud. Why was this perfume not sold and the money given to the poor? The writers make it clear that those who criticized her were not concerned about the poor. Is that not what Jesus means when he reminds them that the poor are always plentiful in an empire economy. The rich get richer and the poor get poorer. If they were really concerned, they would be standing with Jesus in support of the poor and marginal people.

The woman's generosity showed up their greed. She did "a beautiful thing to me" Mark 14:6. Jesus knew that she had anointed him for death. It was a beautiful act and deed of service. As these studies move toward the death and resurrection of Jesus watch for the faithful, courageous acts of the women who followed Jesus. As has been said so often, they were the last at the cross and the first to the empty tomb. This Mary was one of the closest persons to Jesus. She listened, believed and acted. That is what following Jesus means to this day.

Jesus made a very interesting statement. Listen to Jesus, in Mark 14:9 and in Matthew 26:13, "I tell you the truth, where ever the gospel is preached throughout the world, what she has done will also be told, in memory of her." Recall what she did as we move in the next study to Jesus' Last Meal with His Disciples (before his death). At that meal Jesus will perform the act of washing the disciple's feet. You see, the act of Mary to Jesus and of Jesus to his disciples is a servant's act, washing the feet of guests.

Mary learned her lesson well. A major teaching of Jesus by word and deed was and is servant leadership. You lead by serving. It is a difficult lesson to learn. It takes a lot of practice. Read Mark 10:35-45 to refresh your memory.

Application to Life

Consider how eating with others can break down barriers. How do meals strengthen good relationships? You might want to do this study with friends during a meal together.

Ask yourself which is most important in your life, money and things or persons and relationships? What does Mary's act say to us about thanking people while they are living?

Mary was playing the role of a servant as well as a loving follower of Jesus. How do your life and actions display be a servant? Look how the servant idea and looking toward the death of Jesus in this study foreshadow the events in the next study on Jesus' Last Meal with His Disciples. To prepare that study read Matthew 26:17-30; Mark 14:12-26; Luke 22:7-38; John 13:1-38 and 14:1.

Jesus' Last Meal with His Disciples
Matthew 26:17-30; Mark 14:12-26; Luke 22:7-38; John 13:1-38; 14:1-31

The Bible passages for this study tell of one of the most sacred Christian rituals. It is called by various names; Eucharist, Lord's Supper, Holy Communion. These passages tell us that Jesus gathered his disciples for a last meal. The meal was the Passover meal. It is evident that Jesus had made plans fora room. He gave only two of the disciples the task of watching for a man carrying a water pot who would lead them to the room. (Usually water pots were carried by women). This sounds secretive. Was Jesus making sure that Judas did not know until time for the meal? Mark's home was in Jerusalem. Do you suppose he is the one carrying the pot of water? Plans for the Passover meal were carried out.

You may recall that the Passover celebration was a Jewish festival. Jesus was a Jew. The Passover celebrated the deliverance of the Jews from Egyptian bondage by Moses. During this meal Jesus began a ritual that would symbolize deliverance for all of creation from the bondage of sin and its path to death.

If you have not already read the Bible passages, please do so now. You may have noticed several conversations and things happening. For this study, four of those will be briefly considered. To help you to remember the events and the seeming order, think about: The Traitor; The Towel; The Table; The Testament; The Teacher.

Jesus knew that his time had come to face the religious and civic leaders who opposed him. He some way knew that Judas had made a deal with the authorities to lead them to Jesus. So, the nonviolent Jesus ate the deliverance meal with the one who sold him out. Before being too condemning of Judas, note that before the night is over all the disciples will deny knowing Jesus and/or flee when Jesus is taken into custody. Could Judas have been trying to force Jesus to take up arms against the enemy? It is evident in many of the past studies in this Story of Jesus that very few, if any, could accept that Jesus, if he was the Christ, would be killed. The common idea of the Christ was that he would be a military king.

It was a servant's job to wash the feet of guests. Jesus, as the host, took a towel. By washing and drying the disciples' feet, Jesus was teaching them a lesson in service. He said the disciples should wash one another's feet. Did he mean literally to wash each other's feet? Why not? Pope Frances did in 2015. Many think it was an act of symbolism indicating that disciples should act in the spirit of servants to others. Yes, surely it means that. This is what it means to love one another. So, two lessons so far; be loyal even when you don't understand and be a serving disciple.

At the table of the Passover meal Jesus took a loaf of bread, blessed it, broke it and gave it to the disciples. They were instructed to eat it. It represented his body which was given for the whole world. He took a cup or chalice of wine, blessed it, and gave it to the disciples. Each was to drink from the cup. The wine represented Jesus' blood. It was to be shed for all mankind. They were to do this often. Some think it should be every meal? It was to remind them of Jesus' death. They were to know their discipleship was to follow Jesus in loyal, nonviolent devotion. They were to look forward to the coming of the consummation of God's Kingdom.

Some say the supper was a testament in his blood. That is true. But also, read John 13:34-35, "A new command I give you: Love one another. As I have loved you, so you must love one another. By this all men will know that you are my disciples, if you love one another." Love God and love others. Those are the two great commands. They just keep coming up in the Old Testament and the New Testament.

Read John 14 again. One of the most comforting and assuring passage in the Bible. Jesus speaks words of comfort and encouragement to the disciples. In fact, the word translated Counselor could be translated encourager, one called alongside to help. Read verse 26, "But the Counselor, the Holy Spirit, whom the Father will send in my name, will **teach** you all things and will remind you of everything I have said to you."

Application to Life

Read and reread the John passages; so much there to live by. Look for the comfort and promises: preparing a place, coming again, and so much more. Think about and discuss the five T words in this study. How does each speak to how a follower of Jesus should live? Consider observing the Eucharist and washing feet with your group or family.

Part 8

The Trials And Crucifixion Of Jesus

Jesus in the Garden of Gethsemane
Matthew26:30-46; Mark 14:26-42;
Luke 22:39-46 John 18:1

A preview of the seven events in this section of the study of the Story of Jesus may be helpful. Following his last meal with the disciples in Part 7 of the study, Jesus led the disciples up the Mount of Olives. They went to a garden area called Gethsemane to pray. It is believed that Jesus often went there for prayer. In the second study of part 8 Jesus was betrayed and arrested in Gethsemane.

Third study, Jesus was tried before the Jewish high court called the Sanhedrin. Fourth, Jesus was tried before Pilate, the Roman Governor of Judea. Fifth, Jesus carried his cross to Golgotha. Sixth, Jesus was crucified. Seventh, Jesus was buried.

The Mount of Olives towered above the Temple mount by about 200 feet. Many olive trees were on the mountain. Jesus seems to have begun his entry into Jerusalem on the donkey, from the Mount of Olives (Matthew 22:1). He ascended from there (Acts 1). That will be the last study in the story, Part 9 study 6. In this study consider the deep human emotions of Jesus; Jesus' prayer; and Jesus word to his disciples.

Jesus knows that even his closest disciples had not grasped his nonviolent mission of love. They were confused. Surely, they were wondering why he had not formed his followers into an army of rebels. Why he had told them he was going to Jerusalem and would be killed. Was he not to be a king like King David who was king of Israel nine centuries before? What is the meaning of a dying Christ? Jesus knew that one of his own, Judas, would on that very night, betray him. He knew that the other eleven disciples would deny him and run. That is enough to cause deep emotion. Look for the words of emotion used by the writers as they described the feelings Jesus had: "deeply distressed and troubled," "overwhelmed with sorrow to the point of death" (Mark 14:33,34). Do you think Jesus was disappointed that the disciples did not understand? Do you think he had dread for the time when they would all desert him? How do you think you would feel in his place? He knew that the temple police and religious leaders were on their way. Death seemed certain and soon. Jesus was a human being. Can you imagine how he was feeling? Stop reading, close your eyes and try to imagine how you might have felt.

Do you see two parts in Jesus' prayer? "If it is possible let this cup pass." Is there another way that love can be shown without suffering the cross? Jesus came to reveal how much God loves his creation, including human kind. Jesus had revealed that love through mercy and compassion. He had stood firm with the poor and suffering against the power, pride, greed and possessions of the ruling class, both religious and civil. They seemed to be in control, but the end would show that God's way even defeats death. The second part of the prayer is, "Not my will, but your will be done." He surrendered to the way of suffering to show the heart of the loving God; his forgiveness and the WAY to abundant life. He entered the suffering of humans and would die. What mercy, forgiveness, and love he showed for all the people of the world.

It seems Jesus had taken all eleven to the mount. He had told them to pray. Trials lay ahead. Then he took Peter, James and John some distance more. He left them with the words to watch and pray. But they fell asleep. Twice after praying, Jesus came back to find them sleeping. One gospel says they slept because of sorrow. Surely, they were worried, scared, exhausted. They fell asleep. Stop and consider their situation instead of being critical of them. Remember a time when you could not stay awake. It may have been a time when it was dangerous, like driving or keeping watch. No doubt they were upset with themselves. Jesus waked them the third time and leads them to meet the arresting posse.

Application to Life

Discuss the two parts of Jesus' prayer. Have you prayed for something not to happen, yet it did? How difficult is it for you to pray, "Thy will be done?" Be careful how you blame God when things don't go as you wish. That is be careful about saying, "It was God's will that this happened." How do you know something is God's will?

Jesus Was Betrayed and Arrested
Matthew 26:47-56; Mark 14:43-52;
Luke 22:47-53; John 18:2-12

Jesus had his last meal with the disciples. There he had established a new ritual, called The Eucharist or Lord's Supper or Holy Communion. The bread and wine were to be reminders of his body and blood at the crucifixion. They were to represent his continuing presence with them. They were told to take the elements as a remembrance and a reminder of the hope they had in Jesus.

Then Jesus led the disciples to a garden called Gethsemane, on the Mount of Olives. During this time, Judas had gone to get those with whom he had bargained to betray Jesus. Judas knew that Jesus would go to Gethsemane as was his custom (John 18:2). It is at this point that this study of the betrayal and arrest of Jesus begins. Consider three divisions as you read the Bible passages listed above: Jesus was betrayed by Judas; Jesus responded to his captors; and his disciples reacted with fear.

Jesus had had time for prayer and was talking with the disciples when the arresting posse came. It consisted of Jewish religious leaders, the temple guard or police, and, according to John's account, Roman soldiers. There is debate as to how many, but it is agreed by scholars that there was a crowd. They were armed with swords, staves, and torches. It was as though they were coming to battle a host of armed soldiers. Rather than flee, Jesus went to meet them, asked them who they were looking for, and told them he was the one. The guards fell to the ground. Fear? Were they expecting a fight? Judas went up to Jesus and kissed him. A greeting for a friend was his sign to the guards which one was Jesus. Jesus asked, "Are you betraying me with a kiss? "What about Judas? Did he think Jesus would resist, maybe call down a host of angels to destroy his enemy? Was Judas so disappointed with Jesus' nonviolent way that he betrayed him? Soon after this, Judas returned the money paid for betrayal and took his own life. May God have mercy on him.

Jesus stood fearless in the presence of those who were out to have him killed. He acted very surprised that the religious leaders of such high standing would stoop to such tactics. Coming at night, with torches, swords, clubs, temple guards and soldiers. They came as though to arrest a fugitive, a murderer, a whole band of outlaws. He reminded them that he had been teaching all week in daylight at the temple. Why wait till middle of the night? Of course, Jesus knew the answer that they dare not admit to him. They were afraid of the people, the crowds liked Jesus. Had they arrested Jesus in public, the crowds may have caused a riot. A riot would not be permitted by Pilate, the Roman governor of Judea. The religious leaders were afraid of losing their prestige, power and possessions. Jesus showed tremendous bravery in the way he faced the arrest. Picture the man Jesus, self-controlled, Spirit controlled, God controlled, word it as you like. Nonviolently he stood his ground before the violent powers of his day, civil and religious. There is a lesson there.

The immediate response of Peter was anger and fight. He drew a sword and attempted to decapitate a servant of the high priest. Did the man dodge? Peter only got his ear. Luke wrote that Jesus healed the ear and told Peter to put the sword away. He commented, "No more of this" Luke 22:51. "Put your sword back in its place, for all who draw the sword, will die by the sword" Matthew 26:52 Civilization has yet to understand and live by Jesus' statement. Then all the disciples fled Matthew 26:56.

An interesting addition is made by Mark. "A young man, wearing nothing but a linen garment, was following Jesus. When they seized him, he fled naked, leaving his garment behind." Mark 14:51-52. Who was this young man? Many think it could have been Mark, the writer of the Gospel of Mark. Was the last supper in an upper room of Mary, Mark's mother's home? Can't you imagine her son, Mark, (teen?), being curious about what was going on? Can't you see him slipping out the window with only a sheet or sleeping garment? See him following Jesus and the disciples to the garden of Gethsemane and getting caught in the arresting process? No way to know, but it is a possibility. Mark at least knew about it and put it in his Jesus story.

Application to Life

Jesus stood firm and nonviolent when faced with the hate of those who loved position, power, possessions more than God. How you are to think, speak and act toward those same forces in your society? The disciples reacted with fear, anger, fight and flight. These reactions make you become like those you fear. Read the Sermon of the Mount and James. They speak of faith, love and common good of all.

Jesus Before Annas and the Sanhedrin
Matthew 26:57-75; Mark 14:53-75;
Luke 22:54-71; John 18:12-27.

This study, along with the nine preceding and seven studies to follow, deals with Jesus' last week or "Holy Week" as it is called in the Christian calendar. The eight days began when Jesus entered Jerusalem riding a donkey (Palm Sunday). The eight days ends the following Sunday when Jesus was raised from death and made appearances to his disciples. The current study takes place on what our time would call Thursday evening and early Friday morning.

Read the above passages at the beginning of this study. Look for three "trials" before Jewish religious authorities. In the next study you will discover three more "trials" before the Roman civil court. Trials are put in quotation marks because much of what took place is a mockery of any justice system.

In this study Jesus was taken to stand before Annas, the former high priest. Then he appeared before Caiaphas and other Jewish religious leaders. Finally, after day break the Sanhedrin met to pronounce a guilty verdict. The story of Peter denying that he knew Jesus was a disciple of Jesus is included in the religious trials, as you just noted in the passages.

Jesus was taken by the arresting temple guards to Annas, according to John. "Then the detachment of soldiers with its commander and the Jewish officials arrested Jesus. They bound him and brought him first to Annas, who was the father-in-law of Caiaphas, the high priest that year" John 18:12-13. The other gospel writers say that Jesus was taken to the home of the high priest. This raises the question: Did Annas live with his son-in-law? It also raises a "power behind the throne" question. Annas had not been high priest since the year 15 or 16 A.D. Was he still the decision maker through Caiaphas? When questioned about his teaching, Jesus told Annas to ask those present. They had heard Jesus teach. Jesus had taught openly in the temple court in broad daylight. There may be implication or even accusation by Jesus here about an illegal night time questioning with no defense testimony. Jesus is reprimanded by a guard for lack of respect for

Annas. Again, was Jesus answer that he did not know the high priest a factual statement. Or was he saying that Annas was not now high priest and had not been for about 15 years? They take Jesus next to Caiaphas.

Caiaphas had sought and brought witnesses to accuse Jesus. But they could not find two, as required by Old Testament law, to agree. Their attempt was to use Jesus' statement, "We heard him say," 'I will destroy this man-made temple and in three days will build another, not made by man" Mark 14:58. Though they could not agree on what Jesus had said or meant. Jesus was finally asked if he was the Messiah. He replied, "I am." That became the crime, blasphemy, of which Jesus would be charged. They want a death penalty. They will need Roman help. They will take Jesus to Pilate, the Roman governor.

But first they abuse Jesus with strikes, slaps and spittle. He is made fun of. The whole thing, from beginning to end, was a farce.

The verdict had been decided; but, to make things "legal" the Sanhedrin was called into session after day light. Trial by night was illegal. You may want to check your Bible dictionary on the trials of Jesus to find how many laws were broken to indict an innocent Jesus. The Sanhedrin consisted of seventy members, Sadducees, Pharisees, scribes, and lawyers. It was the supreme court of the Jewish people. It was made up of elite persons; persons who had money, power, prestige and leaned toward Roman rule, in order to keep the before mentioned privileges. The court simply gave a daylight stamp of approval. Then they took Jesus to Pilate. That is the next study. To conclude this study, look at the denials of Peter.

Peter enters the courtyard of the high priest with the help of another disciple, believed by many to be John. Peter, as Jesus had predicted, denied Jesus three times. At least one denial took place near a charcoal fire. Such a fire will be referred to in a later study. Can you imagine how Peter felt when the cock crew, as Jesus had predicted. If that is bad, think how he felt when Jesus was led from the trial and looked at Peter. Peter wept in regret and repentance. But God will use this to change a weak Simon into Peter the rock.

Application to Life

Think about and discuss the "errors" in the trials. How do the courts of justice work in your country? Are religious persons influenced by money, power, prestige, position? What about yourself. How do you make personal judgments about people? Do all people have to agree with you? Do you think Jesus demonstrated nonviolence in the face of violence? Did he show love for those who wanted him killed? What about Peter? Was he overconfident in his own power? When have you not spoken up for someone being falsely accused? Have you denied being Christian? Why?

Jesus Before Governor Pilate
Matthew 27:1-26; Mark 15:1-15;
Luke 23:1-25; John 18:28-40; 19:1-16

In the previous study there were three "trials" of Jesus before the religious leaders. In this study there are three "trials" before civil and political authorities. Watch for two trials before Pilate, governor of Judea and one before Herod, puppet king of Galilee, Jesus' home territory. Recall in the previous study the religious leaders had determined to have Jesus killed. But they had difficulty getting their witnesses against Jesus to agree on their accusations. They decided that their best claim was Jesus blasphemed by claiming to be God's son. Watch, as you read the scripture for this study (listed above), how they change their claim. Pilate, as a civil and Roman governor, would care less about what Jesus' religious claims were. They needed a criminal, political claim in order to have Jesus crucified.

So, Jesus was taken to Pilate. Pilate sent him to Herod. Herod sent Jesus back to Pilate. If you have not done so, now is the time to read carefully the scripture passages above. Note that Mark and Matthew are almost alike. Luke adds the trial before Herod and John adds additional information. Recall that each writer was writing at a different time, to a different audience and each may have had different sources Pilate's headquarters were in Caesarea on the coast of the Mediterranean Sea. He had come to Jerusalem to insure against any rioting during the Passover festival. This was convenient for the religious leaders to bring Jesus before Pilate and present their case against Jesus. They needed to change their charge from blasphemy to traitor of Rome.

The change of charge was that Jesus claimed to be king of the Jews. They said that he was telling the Jews not to pay their taxes to Rome. Now, this could have really gotten Pilate's attention. But Pilate seemed to see through their plan and knew from the beginning that they had come because of jealousy and personal prestige problems. He seemed to see Jesus as no threat to Rome. Keep in mind that Pilate was a politician. His main concern was keeping peace and protecting his job.

Note the irony in the trials; the religious leaders refused to go into Pilate's house for fear of defiling themselves religiously. No problem with killing an innocent man with whom they disagreed but keep themselves undefiled for temple attendance. Pilate thought of a way to rid himself of the whole matter. He knew that Herod, puppet king of Galilee, was in Jerusalem for the Passover. Pilate learned that Jesus was from Galilee, so he sent Jesus to Herod.

Luke told us this part of the story. Herod had heard of Jesus and was curious and eager to meet him. Herod hoped to see a miracle performed by Jesus. As before Pilate, Jesus remained silent. Herod's soldiers abused and mocked Jesus. Herod sent him back to Pilate with the message that he could find no fault with Jesus. Note in all four gospel stories how often Jesus remained silent. And how few words he used when he spoke.

Pilate made them an offer. It was a custom at the festival to release a Jewish prisoner. Pilate offered Jesus Barabbas, a real villain or Jesus who is called Christ. The accusers of Jesus chose Barabbas to be released. Pilate asked what he should do with Jesus. They cried out that he should be crucified. Pilate was running out of ideas and too much a coward to take a stand for justice. It may have been about this time that word was brought to Pilate from his wife. She had a nightmare and urged Pilate to have nothing to do with this trial. Was it at this point that Pilate washed his hands as a symbolic way of saying he was through? But the crowd insisted. Pilate's final tactic was to have Jesus flogged, a beating that often-caused death. He brought the beaten and bleeding Jesus before them and asked what they thought. They cried again for Jesus to be crucified. Pilate caved, the soldiers mocked Jesus with royal clothes and a crown of thorns. They jeered and tormented him. They would lead him to Calvary.

This whole ordeal was filled with irony. He is not only King of the Jews, but of all of creation. Somewhere in the mystery of all this is the truth that love is stronger than hate. Jesus willingly suffered humiliation unto death and through it became Victor.

Application to Life

Think about and discuss how jealousy or envy can distort your ideas about others. Does your position, prestige, power, privilege distort your practice of treating all persons with justice and equality? When is it more appropriate to be silent than to speak? How open are you to persons of other religions or faiths? Do you think Jesus actions were stronger than words could have been? Think of someone who thinks different from you. Be kind to that person this week.

Jesus Was Led to Golgotha
Matthew 27:27-34; Mark 15:16-23; Luke 23:26-32; John 19:17

A lot can change in a few days. Remember the parade in Part 7, study 1? It was about Jesus' Triumphal Entry into Jerusalem on the Sunday before the present study which took place on Friday. Reread Mark 11:1-11 to refresh your memory. Now refresh your memory by reviewing in your mind what happened to this present study: Jesus Cleansed the Temple; Some Greeks met Jesus; Rulers Tried to Trap Jesus; Jesus Taught the Disciples that the Temple would be Destroyed; He ate with Simon the Leper and was anointed by a Woman; Jesus Instituted the Lord's Supper; He Prayed in Gethsemane; He was Betrayed and Arrested; He had three "trials "before the religious leaders and three "trials' before political leaders and condemned to be crucified. What a week, and it was not over. In this study Jesus was led to Golgotha to be crucified. A foreigner was conscripted to carry Jesus' cross and Jesus gave a last warning to the women who followed.

Note the contrast of this parade to the one on the preceding Sunday. Sunday he **entered Jerusalem** with a crowd proclaiming him as Messiah. On Friday Jesus **exited Jerusalem** with two criminals and soldiers who would crucify him. On Sunday the crowds were **singing.** On Friday women followers were **weeping** and the crowd was **deriding him**. On Sunday Jesus was thought to be **the Christ** by many but on Friday many of those watching thought him to be a **criminal.**

Scholars say, those condemned to crucifixion by Roman power were forced to carry their own cross to the place of crucifixion. Some say the upright part of the cross was set permanently at the site; the victim carried the horizontal cross beam. There was a custom for a placard to be carried before the victim stating his crime. This would give fair warning to all who watched what happens to one guilty of said crime. Jesus' placard read, Jesus of Nazareth King of the Jews. Did Pilate write the sign in jest toward the Jews, not knowing the truth he was proclaiming? Note that it was written in three languages according to John 19:19-22.

Because of the beating and endurance of hours of mock trials and ridicule, Jesus was exhausted. He must have struggled with the weight of the cross. The soldiers conscripted Simon from Cyrene in Africa to carry Jesus Cross.

Countee Cullen wrote about it. You can find her poems on you computer or at your library.

Interesting, it was the women followers who dared follow the parade to Calvary. Surely some of them had been in the triumphal parade on the preceding Sunday. Now they are weeping. Their dreams have been dashed. The Christ they loved was facing death. They wept. Jesus told them not to weep for him, but for Jerusalem. Again, he predicted, as he had to the disciples in Mark 13, Jerusalem was going to be destroyed. The woe is not against child bearing, but that it will be an awful time for all when the Romans destroy the holy city. It happened some forty years later in 70 A.D.

Application to Life

Discuss the contrasts between the two parades. Note the nonviolent vs. the violent. Imagine where you would have been during the Via Dolorosa. Discuss the poem. Sing the Via Dolorosa. Discuss how poetry and art speak truth. Discuss ways you can stand with those falsely accused. Does your church seek to aid the families of prisoners?

Jesus on the Cross
Matthew 27:35-56; Mark 15: 24-41, Luke 23:33-49; John 19:18-37

At least six grueling hours of Jesus' death are described in the passages for this study. Take time now to read them slowly and prayerfully. Look for the people who are at the cross and their reactions. Watch for the "seven sayings" of Jesus. There is at least one in each gospel.

There were six persons or groups of persons at Calvary:

Two criminals were crucified with Jesus. Both are said to have ridiculed Jesus. But one had a change of mind and asked to be remembered by Jesus. Jesus promised that he would be with him in paradise.

The crowd and the religious leaders were there to continue their mocking and ridicule. Note the varied accusations repeated from the mock trials.

The soldiers were there to do their job. They also took Jesus' clothes and divided them among themselves. A fifth garment they gambled for. One soldier recognized Jesus as the Son of God.

The women and followers, according to one gospel, viewed from a distance. At least Mary, his mother, and other women must have been as close as possible. Mary is said by some to represent all the Mary's of the New Testament.

John and the disciples were there. Do you think the disciples were all there or just John? Are they the ones that are standing afar off? (Luke 23:19) John placed himself at the cross near Jesus' mother.

The Seven Sayings of Jesus Can we be sure which order the sayings were in?

1) "My God, my God, why have you forsaken me?" This is a quote from Psalm 22. Was Jesus quoting the entire psalm? Did Jesus really feel forsaken? Why not? Would not you have felt forsaken in his place? The son of man was fully human and experienced the darkness of aloneness.

2) "Father forgive them, they don't know what they are doing." Amazing grace! Was this forgiveness for the ones crucifying him? Yes. Was the forgiveness for the whole world? Yes. Then he came to save us all.

3) "Today you will be with me in Paradise."

This was Jesus' response to the criminal who said to Jesus, "Remember me when you come into your kingdom." This is another identification of Jesus with lost humanity.

4) **"Woman behold thy son; son behold thy mother."(John 19:25-27)** In his dying Jesus did not forget the one who loved him more than any other human being. He saw that she was cared for by the one who called himself the beloved disciple.

5) "I thirst."(John 19:28) Remember that Jesus suffered as a human being.

6) "It is finished."(John 19:30) Was Jesus speaking of his mission? Was Jesus saying he had finished the business that he referred to as a 12-yearold in a temple?

Is he saying that he finished the mission he began when he was baptized by John the Baptist? Is he saying that he finished the mission he committed himself to during the temptation experience in Matthew 4?

7) "Into your hands I commit my spirit."(Luke 23:46)

Reactions to the Crucifixion

Nature reacted with darkness. The curtain in the temple was torn in part from top to bottom indicating God's openness to all people. The centurion reacted by saying, "Surely this was the Son of God." And Matthew said that graves were opened, and dead people walked. Was this metaphor?

Application to Life

Meditate for five minutes on the suffering of love in life and death. Make notes of Jesus' suffering both in life and in death. Jesus death shows how much God loves the whole world. Jesus life and death reveal the character of God. Jesus did not come to change God's idea about man, but to change man's idea of God.

Jesus Was Buried
Matthew 27:57-66; Mark 15:42-47; Luke 23:50-56; John 19:31-42

Read the passages listed above at the beginning of this study. Look for the persons participating and what each did. Pray for understanding.

Following Jesus' death on the cross, Joseph, from the Jewish town of Arimathea, asked Pilate for permission to bury Jesus' body. Pilate granted the permission after learning from the soldier in charge of the crucifixion that Jesus was indeed dead.

The boldness of Joseph's request is evident, in that, though he was a member of the Jewish council (Sanhedrin) that condemned Jesus, Joseph did not assent to the decision.

It seems to have been the custom that bodies of the crucified were left hanging on their crosses for at least two reasons. One was so those passing by would see what happens to those who rebelled against Rome. A second reason was so that the vultures and wild animals would eat the flesh from the bones of those crucified. Joseph request to bury Jesus was an act of mercy and compassion. John's Gospel tells that Nicodemas also participated in Jesus burial. See John chapter three for the story of the Pharisee coming to Jesus one night and learned about being "born again" or born from above. Nicodemas was also a member of the Jewish council that condemned Jesus. He and Joseph must have been brave men. Nicodemas brought seventy-five pounds of a mixture of myrrh and aloes. They wrapped Jesus' body with the spices in strips of linen cloth and placed him in the grave. See John 19:39-40.

The grave where they buried Jesus belonged to Joseph. It was a hole cut in a huge stone with another stone to block the entrance or close the grave. It was near the place of crucifixion.

Some of the Jewish leaders asked that Pilate station guards at the grave. Was their reason that Jesus had predicted that he would rise from the dead? They gave Pilate the reason that they were afraid that

Jesus' disciples would come and steal his body from the grave. So, Pilate did as request. He sent soldiers to guard the tomb of Jesus. And he had the "door" of the tomb sealed with his seal.

The women were there watching and grieving at the cross and the grave. They observed what was done by Joseph and Nicodemas. Then they returned to the place where they were staying. They planned to return after the Sabbath and anoint the body of Jesus.

There is a saying that "a picture is worth a thousand words." At this point in your study take time to look at the picture called The Pieta. It is marble sculpture by Michelangelo. It depicts Mary holding the body of her son, Jesus. The work was done in 1498-1499. It is 174 cm. x 195 cm. or 68.5 in x 76.8 in. It is in St Peter's Basilica in Rome. It is the only piece Michelangelo ever signed. It is said that he was so embarrassed that he had signed it that he never signed another work.

Application to Life

Think about and discuss with your group ways the Joseph and Nicodemas showed sympathy and compassion for Jesus and his followers. What do you learn from their actions that you and your study group or church could do for others in their time of grief?

Find and study a picture or small sculptured depiction of the Pieta. Try to imagine the feelings of Mary as she holds the body of Jesus.

In present day news and fiction death, killing, execution, war and violence seem to occur with no thought of grief for the victims or compassion for their families. Discuss how you can become more sensitive to such events.

Often compassion is shown for a short time and then those in grief are forgotten. Discuss thing you and your group can do to follow up with grieving persons or families. Maybe mark on your calendar dates to remember those who have had loses. Your church may want to begin a grief recovery group. Study grief and how to help those with emotions that can accompany grief.

Women Came to Jesus' Tomb
Matthew 28:1-15; Mark 16:1-11;
Luke 24:1-12; John 20:1-18

"He is risen!" "He is risen, indeed!" This is the greeting and response used by the early church on Easter morning. It is often still used by many today. Easter is the annual celebration of the church to commemorate the resurrection of Jesus.

Glory! Some thirty hours ago in our scripture study time line Jesus was being buried in the empty tomb of Joseph. The grave was sealed, and Roman soldiers stationed there to make sure no one could steal the body of Jesus and say he rose from the dead. But on Sunday morning the grave was empty. Jesus had risen from the dead!

The apostle Paul wrote to the church in Corinth about the resurrection several years before the four gospels were written. Read what he had to say before moving to the four accounts in the gospels.

For what I received I passed on to you as of first importance: that Christ died for our sins according to the Scriptures; that he was buried; that he was raised on the third day according to the Scriptures, and that he appeared to Peter, and then to the Twelve. After that, he appeared to more than five hundred of the brothers at the same time, most of whom are still living, though some have fallen asleep. Then he appeared to James, then to all the apostles, and last of all he appeared to me also, as to one abnormally born. I Corinthians 15:3-8.

The gospel passages listed above for this study tell how the women who followed Jesus were the first to come and find the empty tomb of Jesus. They came to anoint his dead body but found an empty tomb. So, they became the first evangels. They were the ones sent to tell; the good news, Jesus was alive; risen from the dead.

Matthew tells that Mary Magdalene and another Mary were the first to discover the tomb of Jesus empty. They were told by an angel not to be afraid. Would you not have been afraid at the sight of an angel and Jesus body not in the grave? The angel had rolled the stone door away from the entrance and sat upon it. He informed them that Jesus was not there, and they were to go and tell the other disciples. When they left the tomb, they met Jesus. He also told them not to be afraid and to go tell the disciples that he would meet them in Galilee.

Matthew also indicated phenomena like an earthquake, graves being opened, and dead people being resuscitated. Could Matthew have seen the resurrection of Jesus being the beginning of a whole world being recreated?

Mark said three women went to the tomb. They were Mary Magdalene, Salome, and Mary the mother of James. The tomb was open and an angel inside. The ladies went inside and were told to fear not but go and tell Peter and the disciples that Jesus was going ahead of them to Galilee. Why do you think Jesus would single out Peter to be told? Some believe that Mark got much of his gospel material from Peter.

Luke's story is much the same, except there are two men inside the tomb. They reminded them that Jesus had told his followers that he would rise from the dead. The women returned to tell the disciples, but the disciples did not believe them. Peter did run to the tomb and wondered what had happened. The women listed by Luke, who went to the tomb are Mary Magdalene, Mary mother of James and Joanna.

John wrote that Mary Magdalene told the disciples that Jesus was not in the tomb. He wrote that he (John) and Peter ran to the tomb and discovered for themselves that Jesus was not there. John then recorded a special appearance of Jesus to Mary Magdalene. Reread the conversation of Jesus with Mary. Could Jesus have been saying to her that she could not cling to him bodily, but he would be with her in spirit as she continued to follow him? Did you note that Mary Magdalene in listed in all four of the gospel records of who went to the tomb? Why do you suppose that was done?

Application to Life

Note in all four gospel accounts of Jesus' resurrection women are the ones who go to the grave? Was it only because they had the task of anointing his body? Why do all four accounts list Mary Magdalene? Why did Jesus appear to her first? Do Jesus appearances to the women have anything to say to the status of women in your society? Do you think that Jesus saw them as equal with men? Do you feel good that they were first to tell the good news of Jesus' resurrection?

Part 9

The Resurrection Appearances And Ascension Of Jesus

Jesus Appeared to Two Disciples on the Road to Emmaus
Mark 16:12-13; Luke 24:13-35

In the previous study Jesus appeared to Mary Magdalene and she did not recognize him until he called her name. On the same day Jesus appeared to two disciples, one whose name was Cleopas. Who was the other? Do you think it could have been his wife? Or was it another man? By the invitation in the story for Jesus to have the evening meal with them, it could have been his wife. Note also, as you read the passages listed above from your Bible, that Jesus was not recognized by those two disciples until he blessed and broke bread with them. Could this be Clopas and wife mentioned in John 19:25?

This study will be in three parts: Jesus joins the two disciples as a stranger; Jesus interprets Scripture concerning the Messiah (Christ); Jesus reveals himself to them in the breaking of bread.

Emmaus was about seven miles from Jerusalem. From the story we gather that they had been to Jerusalem for the Passover (Jewish celebration of Moses leading the Jewish people from Egyptian slavery). Sometime the two had become followers or disciples of Jesus. They had hoped, as many, that he would deliver Israel from Roman rule. That had not happened, and Jesus had been killed. Word was that some women went to the tomb, found it empty, and some others went and confirmed their story.

Give some thought to the fact that these two disciples were suffering from grief at the death of Jesus. They had great disappointment in their loss of hope. Yet, they seemed to welcome this stranger to travel with them. They shared their grief with him. The New Testament Book of Hebrews says in chapter thirteen, verse 2, "Do not forget to entertain strangers, for by so doing some people have entertained angels without knowing it." A similar thing happened in this story.

Jesus seems a little put out with the two for their lack of understanding. In fact, all the disciples seemed to have been of a similar mind. Jesus begins to interpret the Hebrew Bible (the Christian Old Testament) passages that have to do with the hoped-for Messiah or Christ. There are many such passages. Luke does not tell us which ones Jesus used. Would he have quoted from Isaiah 61? That is the passage Jesus read to his home town Synagogue at the beginning of his ministry. See Luke 4:17-19. Might he have quoted Ezekiel 34:23-24 and Psalm 23 to remind them Messiah was the Good Shepherd John 10:11? What about a prophet like Moses, read Deuteronomy 18:15-19 and Matthew 21:11. Read any of the gospel accounts of the crucifixion and then Isaiah chapter 53. Whichever he used they still did not recognize him or yet understand.

Night was approaching, and as good Jewish hospitality required, the two insisted Jesus remain for supper and sleep. It was in that experience of Jesus at supper, blessing and breaking bread with them, that their recognition of who he was came to them. And then he disappeared. He walked with them as a stranger, but they did not recognize him. He interpreted Scripture, yet they did not recognize him. But when he blessed and broke bread the light came on.

Do you think those two disciples had been present one of the times Jesus fed a multitude with so little, as in John chapter 6? Is it possible they had been at least looking on as Jesus broke bread with the twelve? There are so many lessons to draw from this passage. Please do more study on the Lord's Supper. The mystery of suffering seen as wine from crushed grapes. Grain made into bread after being ground into powder. A grain of corn dies to produce a crop. Jesus died so there can be resurrection for all.

Their hearts burned, the two disciples would say later, of the scripture interpretation and Jesus walking with them on the road. What about you? Do you recognize that the Spirit of Jesus is walking with you right now?

Application to Life

Take some time to meditate on the fact that God loves you.

They hurried to tell others. You can do that also. Use a Bible Dictionary or other Bible study help to find other Messianic passages to study. Remember, Jesus knew the Hebrew Bible.

Participate in the Lord's Supper and recall the two disciples experience.

Invite some friends and strangers to break bread with you.

Jesus Appeared to the Disciples
Mark 16:14; Luke 24:36-40; John 20:19-31

The stories in the passages for this study took place on the Sunday evening of Jesus' resurrection and one week later. The first story is referred by Mark, Luke and John. John is the only writer to tell the second story, when Thomas was present. In the first story the disciples were gathered behind closed and locked doors. They were afraid, they were grieved. They had lost hope. They were disappointed. But they were together. And the resurrected, living Jesus showed up.

Now, please read the Bible passages for this study, listed above. Look for what Jesus did for those discouraged and frightened disciples. You may find more than are listed below.

Why would they not be afraid? Could not what happened to Jesus, also happen to them? Would not the same "authorities" who trapped Jesus trap them? But Jesus came and spoke his words of **peace** to them. **"Peace be with you."** The same words he had spoken to them on the preceding Thursday evening: **"Peace I** leave with you; my peace I give to you" John 14:27. Can you imagine the calm that they must have felt in the presence of Jesus? Of course, there must have been wonder and fear, also.

Again, why would they not fear and wonder? Their best friend and teacher had been executed. But can you imagine the **joy** they felt when they saw him alive. John said, "The disciples were overjoyed when they saw the Lord." John 20:20. The presence of Jesus brought and brings joy. Followers of Jesus should be joyful.

Those men and women had followed Jesus from Galilee. Some had been with him two or three years. They had learned about the Kingdom of God. They had believed that Jesus was the Messiah, the one to save Israel. They had been part of a mission. Then with Jesus death, there must have been a hopeless feeling. They may have felt like failures. But when Jesus appeared to them, he restored their hope and mission. He gave them hope and purpose. "As the Father has **sent me, I am sending you."** John 20:21. They were given renewed purpose and hope. They had a mission, a Christ given mission.

Along with the other negative feelings, the disciples must have felt helpless, powerless. What do you think? Some of them had cured the sick, had cast out evil spirits. But that was when Jesus was with them. Well, he is back and alive and gives them power. "And with that he breathed on them and said, 'Receive Holy Spirit." John 20:22. Get your Bible and read John chapter fourteen. There Jesus promised this encouraging Spirit of power.

Would you not expect them to have doubts? The Luke passage makes this obvious. John's second story, about Thomas not being present the first Sunday night but came the second Sunday, makes it clear that he had doubts. Jesus told Thomas to look, touch and believe. And so, he did. He received a confession, "My Lord and my God," he said. John 20:28

Application to Life

How does Jesus help you with your negative thoughts and feelings? Does he not promise you and give you what he did to those disciples? Discuss how he does that today: through scripture, prayer, meditation, other persons, opportunity for service, and …. You list other ways.

Jesus Met with Seven Disciples at the Sea of Galilee
John 21:1-26

Please read John 21:1-26 at the beginning of this study. This is the fourth lesson on the appearances of Jesus to his disciples after his resurrection. Two thoughts before discussing the story. Chapter twenty-one appears to be a wonderful after thought of John. If you read the last verse in chapter 20, it seems to be the end of the book. Are you not glad he added chapter twenty-one? Second, though seven disciples went fishing, the major content is about: Jesus and Peter; it is about Jesus appearing to the seven; Jesus' conversation with Peter; and a renewed commission to Peter.

Simon Peter decided to go fishing and six of the other disciples decided to go with him. They fished all night but caught nothing. Jesus appeared on the shore unrecognized. He called to them and asked if they had caught anything. Then he told them to cast the net on the other side of the boat. When they did, they got a net full of fish. John is believed to be the disciple who called himself "the disciple whom Jesus loved." He recognized the man on the shore to be Jesus. He told Peter. Peter put on his garment and jumped into the water to swim to Jesus.

The others came dragging the net that held 153 fish. The count some believe was the number of nations in the world. Jesus had breakfast for the group.

After breakfast Jesus began a conversation with Peter. Three times he asked if Peter loved him (Jesus). Remember how many times Peter had denied knowing Jesus? Right, it was three times. Stop here and read John 18:15-27.

Jesus asked him if he loved Jesus more than "these." Was Jesus talking about boats and fishing? Was he not asking Peter if his love for Jesus was greater than the other disciples? Read the conversation in Mark 14:27-31. Peter made some strong boasts of his loyalty. Peter's responses to Jesus were genuine, but far less boastful now. The point of this story is that Jesus still loved Peter and forgave him.

Try to imagine the feelings of Peter in this story. How did he feel when John told him that the man on the shore was Jesus? What did he think when he saw the huge catch of fish? What were his feelings during breakfast? How did he feel as Jesus questioned him? Was there shame, guilt, joy of renewed fellowship?

Following each of Peter's answers of yes to Jesus question, "Do you love me, Peter," Jesus had given him the commission to feed Jesus' sheep. Peter must have understood Jesus metaphor for caring for God's people. Jesus also predicted that

Peter would die for following him. That was very strong language. History tells that Peter did die by crucifixion. Some say he asked to be crucified upside down because he did not deserve to die upright as Jesus did. Peter saw John near. "What about him (John)?" he asked. Listen carefully to Jesus response, "If I want him to remain alive until I return, what is that to you? You must follow me."

That is the same call that Jesus had given to Peter when he first called him.

Application to Life

Did you notice the use of the five senses (sight, touch, hearing, taste and smell)? Example did John recognize Jesus on the shore by sight, hearing or both. Peter learned it was Jesus by hearing. Imagine the taste and smell of the cooked fish. Think they might have remembered Jesus appearing to them in the locker room and ate fish with them? (See Luke 24:42). There was a charcoal fire on the shore. Peter had warmed himself and smelled the charcoal on the night he denied knowing Jesus. (See John 18:18 and 21:9). In both was a fire of charcoal. Think of times and ways you have learned or been reminded by senses.

Jesus Met with Over 500 Believers in Galilee
Matthew 28:16-20; Mark 16:15-18; I Corinthians 15:6

Please read the suggested Bible passages listed above now. The 500 believers are from the Corinthian passage. Matthew 28:19-20 is one of the best known of saying of Jesus. It is called The Great Commission. The Christian church over the years has understood this commission to be valid for the church through the ages.

All four of the gospel writers had Jesus giving a similar commission. Do you think John meant about the same thing when he recorded Jesus saying, "As the Father has sent me, I am sending you" John 20:21. Luke 24:45-48, "Then he (Jesus) opened their minds so they could understand the Scriptures? He told them, 'This is what is written: The Christ will suffer and rise from the dead on the third day, and repentance and forgiveness of sins will be preached in his name to all nations, beginning at Jerusalem. You are witness of these things. Acts 1:8 has these words of Jesus:

"But you will receive power when the Holy Spirit comes on you and you will be me witnesses in Jerusalem, and in all Judea and Samaria, and to the ends of the earth."

Do you get the feeling that the good news of Jesus is for all people and that his followers are to make it known by word and deed to the whole world? The Good News is that God loves his whole creation and is merciful to forgive all. One Bible study method is to ask the questions: who, what, when, where, and how.

Who Are the People of Jesus' Commission?

Do you think that he meant the 500 who were there with him? What about others who would hear and believe in Jesus later? What about all his followers today? Are yes, yes, and yes, your answers? What about "who" are to be made disciples? Any and all persons everywhere? Sounds like that, doesn't it?

What is the Task of the Commission?

Make disciples of all nations. A disciple is a follower, a learner, a student. You might use other similar words. In this case a follower, learner, student of Jesus. Few better definitions of what as Christian is than one who follows Jesus.

How Are Disciples Made?

To paraphrase the instructions of Saint Francis of Assisi to his disciple: "Everywhere you go preach the good news, if necessary, use words." The commission of Jesus is to be seen in the lives of Jesus followers. Lives that are so lived that others will want to follow Jesus also. This is to be done through the power of the promised Holy Spirit. It is always the Spirit of God who does the converting. Followers are to be baptized. Water baptism signifies that one has decided to follow Jesus; dying to an old way of life and resurrected to a new way. But baptism can also mean being filled or immersed in the Spirit of God. Disciples are to be taught to observe what Jesus taught. The way one lives life speaks so much louder than what is said.

When and Where is the Commission Obeyed?

When is right now and all the time. Where is wherever you are, in all places.

What is the Promise?

Jesus promises his presence now and forever. How often do you think of God as way off and unreachable? Jesus, the Spirit of God is present in the world of his creation and lives within you to help you be what you were created to become.

Application to Life

Discuss how you are obeying The Great Commission. Often this is taken to be work done in other parts of the world. But it means you are a missionary wherever you are. How can you and your group or church improve your mission work? Your answers may have to do with the way you do your daily work, how you relate to others.

Jesus Ascended to Heaven
Mark 16:19-20; Luke 24:50-53; Acts 1:9-12

This is the last of 80 Bible studies on the Story of Jesus. The studies are based on the four Gospels in the New Testament (Matthew, Mark, Luke, John). This final study is about the ascension of Jesus. The ascension is the belief that Jesus was seen returning to his Father, God, from whom he had come into the world. In the first study this coming from God was called the incarnation. That is the belief that God took on human flesh and lived, died and was resurrected. Ascension was forty days after the resurrection. During those days Jesus continued to teach about the Kingdom of God. Ten days later, at Pentecost, the Spirit came upon them.

Only Luke and Mark tell of the ascension, though it is a vital belief, especially for the early disciples. They believed that God was far away in a place called heaven, somewhere in the sky. So, if Jesus came from God and was returning to God, he must go up. Through the teachings of Jesus and the New Testament we come to understand that God is present everywhere and that heaven is more the idea of being with God than some place in the sky. In fact, the New Testament gives strong evidence that God is present and at work in the world he created and is in the process of recreating. Read Romans 8:18-22 and Revelation 21:1-4. So, what does the ascension have to say to us?

Throughout Old Testament history from the time of the Exodus, God had made his presence known by the cloud. A cloud by day and a pillow of fire by night had been over the tabernacle or tent where God met his people. When the cloud moved the people moved. God could speak in the clouds of the storm. How appropriate then, that the disciples saw Jesus ascend on and into the cloud.

There had to be a physical separation. Jesus had explained to them. A body could not be everywhere as could his Spirit. And he had promised that if he went away, back to the Father, he would send his Spirit to be their teacher and encourager. Read John chapter 14 and Acts chapter 2.

The disciples needed to know, following Jesus was not over, it had only begun. Disciples of Jesus today need that assurance also.

Jesus had told them in John 14, that it was necessary for him to go to the Father. But he promised to prepare a place for them and come again to receive them. It is passages like this that give Christians hope for the future. Hope gives courage to those who believe that Christ is still at work in the world through his Spirit. The going away gives hope of his coming again His coming again is not something to be speculated about, but to give courage for living today. Many have led others astray attempting guesses at when Jesus would return. Jesus said even he didn't know. See Mark 13:32.

The final words of commission from Jesus had given his disciples great joy. They had a job to do. Do you remember the last study on The Great Commission? Refresh your memory by reading Matthew 28:16-20and looking ahead read Acts chapters one and two. You can see there that they not only had a task, they were promised power and encouragement by the Spirit of God. Of all people, Christians should be joyful because of the presence of God's Spirit here now and gives hope for the future.

Application to Life

Discuss the mission and responsibility of the first disciples. How does that apply to Jesus' followers today? Do you need to do a review of the nine parts of this study? What plans do you or your group have for your next study and work?

Spend some time meditating on the fact that God's Spirit is with/in you now.

www.ingramcontent.com/pod-product-compliance
Lightning Source LLC
Chambersburg PA
CBHW071309110526
44591CB00010B/833